THE book of CRIMINAL QUOTATIONS

First published in Great Britain in 2003
by Artnik
341b Queenstown Road
London SW8 4LH
UK

ISBN 1 903906 30 X

Cover: Geoff Searle
Design: Mark Lloyd

Printed and bound in Spain by Bookprint

THE book of CRIMINAL QUOTATIONS

Edited ***J.P. Bean***

Contents

J.P. Bean...not a mug shot

Foreword

Somewhere in his Journals Ralph Waldo Emerson writes: "I hate quotations. Tell me what you know." Which is a great quote. I agree that it is irritating for someone to use the words and ideas of others to bolster their own case but, as a working hack, I often do exactly that raiding books of quotations and newspaper listings of sayings of the day to pad out my copy. More times than not the quotes I use are not particularly profound or even insightful. What I love is how the comment of someone sheds light on them, opens up a window into their mind. In this context, even the banal can be fascinating.

Sergei Prokofiev said, "I hate imitation." Which I would argue is a more biting quote than Emerson's. The Book of Criminal Quotations is certainly no imitation...in the words of Norman Selby, it is "The real McCoy". J.P. Bean has scoured the criminal literature and assembled this quite unique compilation. And his book is a first. While the words of criminals often figure in quotation books, Bean is the first editor to produce a book exclusively devoted to what murderers, rapists, robbers... have actually said.

His book also works on a number of levels. It is as one would expect packed with gallow's humour and very funny. Can anyone not laugh at the last words of 13-murders Cherokee Bill Goldsby on the scaffold. His response to the traditional question of whether he had anything to say: "I came here to die, not to make a speech."

Many of the quotes are also shocking, creepy, macabre, horrible; but political, too. These are people who don't believe in the social order – especially its distribution of wealth – and they have acted out their beliefs. Yet, there is also a philosophical vein in many of the quotes that draws on the amoral underpinnings of the human condition. The post-modernist nightmare. We can choose not merely evil but nihilism, and choose it with a relish. When I read some of these quotes, I am reminded of something most of us hide from – there are people out there who are on the prowl for victims to torture, rape and kill just for sheer hell of it. And that is an enduring fact of life. They have always been there and will always be there.

And they are just like you and me.

John McVicar

Who, Me?

Al Capone, *told he was wanted for murder:*

‘Who, me? I’m a respectable business man. I’m a second-hand furniture dealer. I’m no gangster.’

... ‘I am a gambler and a businessman, nothing more. I never robbed a person in my life. I never killed in my life and I never broke into a building or blew open a safe.’

...bemoaning his public image:

‘I’ve never been convicted of a crime, never, nor have I directed anyone else to commit a crime. I don’t pose as a plaster saint but I never killed anyone. And I’m known all over the world as a millionaire gorilla. My wife and my mother hear so much about what a terrible criminal I am, it’s getting too much for them, and I’m sick of it myself. The other day a man came in and said that he had to have three thousand dollars. If I’d give it to him, he said, he’d make me beneficiary in a fifteen thousand dollar insurance policy he’d take out, and then kill himself. I got a letter from a woman in England. She offered me £100 and my passage to London if I’d bump off some neighbours she’d been having a spat with. Even over there I’m known as a gorilla.’

Arnold Rothstein, *known as "The Big Bank Roll" in New York City in the 1920s, on his success:*

"With me it's brains, that's all."

...to reporters outside a Chicago where he had been called to testify in the Black Sox baseball bribery scandal of 1919, which he had masterminded:

"Gentlemen, what kind of courtesy is this? What kind of city is this? I came here voluntarily and what happens? A gang of thugs bar my path with cameras as though I was a notorious person, a criminal even!"

Albert De Salvo, *the Boston Strangler, after his arrest.*

"I've been known as the Cat Man, the Green Man, the Phantom Burglar – and now the Boston "S" Man!"

Denis Nilsen, *the Muswell Hill killer who told police he had murdered "fifteen or sixteen" young men.*

"No one wants to believe, ever, that I am just an ordinary man come to an extraordinary and overwhelming conclusion."

"... I think I am a very rare animal indeed. I don't fit in with the herd. I don't do what other people do, not even in here. I don't watch football matches on television or violent karate films, I don't conform."

"... I have been my own secret scriptwriter, actor, director and cameraman. I took this world of make-believe, where no one really gets hurt, into the real world, and people can get hurt in the real world."

"... I seemed always to travel at 100mph in a stream of traffic with an upward limit of 30mph.

Nobody ever got really got close to me. I was a child of deep romanticism in a harsh plastic functionary materialism....I am an odd personality for today.❞

❝...Now that the Court has accepted the "evidence" that I am God I've begun to get loony letters from religious freaks...all this because I casually threw police a psychiatric cliché. I wonder if the press would print it if I said, "At that moment I really believed I was the Emperor of China." ❞

Legs Diamond, *New York gangster of the 1920s:*

❝I'm just a young fellow trying to get ahead. I never did anything wrong. I wouldn't harm a flea.❞

Legs Diamond, *shortly before he was shot dead.*

❝The bullet hasn't been made that can kill me.❞

Arthur Harding, *turn-of-the-century East End villain who thought nothing of firing a revolver, or of thrusting a glass in the face of adversaries.*

❝As an Englishman, I would never use a knife.❞

Auguste Ricord, *French gangster.*

❝I'm just a prosperous restaurateur. My specialities are meat balls and coquelets a la creme with mushrooms.❞

Charles Manson, *in a statement after his conviction for the Tate-La Bianca murders:*

❝Mr and Mrs America – you are wrong. I am not the King of the Jews nor am I a hippy cult leader. I am what you have made of me and the mad dog devil killer fiend leper is a reflection of your society.

Whatever the outcome of this madness that you call a fair trial or Christian justice, you can know this: In my mind's eye my thoughts light fires in your cities.❞

Arthur Thompson, *Glasgow gangster, asked in court if he was well-known in the city:*

© Chapter Titile

❝I have more cousins than Hitler had an army – everybody claims to know me.❞

Bernard Walden, *a disabled Rotherham lecturer who shot and killed a student and her boyfriend:*

❝I am not as other men. I am a cripple and must be armed to put me on fair terms with others. I have an absolute right to kill.❞

Billy Hill, *on his control over the London underworld in the 1950s:*

❝If you stand in any part of Soho at any hour of the day or night, you will be spotted by at least six of my men. Walk a mile in any direction and you will pass a dozen. This is the centre of my empire, the district from which I rule the underworld of Britain. Walk up Shaftesbury Avenue and ask...who rules the underworld...ask a copper. He'll tell you Billy Hill is the "Guv'nor".❞

...at the Old Bailey, after denying that he considered himself "King of Soho", asked by counsel what title he took for himself if not a kingdom or a dukedom?:

❝The Boss of the Underworld.❞

Jack Spot, *Hill's great rival:*

❝I did what no one else had ever done before. I was the first man to realise that criminals could be organised, each crook becoming a small part of a master plan in which every cog and spindle operated perfectly. I became the planner and the mastermind. I became Boss of the Underworld.❞

Vincenzo Sinagra, *ordered by the Mafia to try to avoid life imprisonment for murder by pretending to be insane:*

❝I never tried to be a lunatic before. How do you be a lunatic?❞

Frank "The Mad Axeman" Mitchell, *after escaping from Rampton and Broadmoor mental institutions, running amok on each occasion:*

❝I do not consider myself insane. I just jumped from the frying pan into the fire.❞

Ronnie Kray, *on a report that he and his brother Reg were to be taxed on the income from their books and film:*

❝How can you ask me to pay any tax? I am a madman.❞

Carlos Lehder, *multi-millionaire drug baron:*

❝I am just a poor Columbian peasant who has made something of himself.❞

William Gillen, *failed Glasgow bank robber, to a witness who failed to pick him out on an identification parade:*

“Don't you recognise me?”

Bugs Moran, *rival of Al Capone in 1920s Chicago, passing a Chicago judge at a ballpark:*

“That's a beautiful diamond ring you're wearing, Your Honour. If it's ever snatched some night, promise you won't go hunting me. I'm telling you now, Judge, that I'm innocent.”

Frank Costello, *Mafia boss known as "The Prime Minister of the Underworld, in an interview with a journalist who asked him if he was a racketeer:*

“If you say I was or am a racketeer, I guess you'll be right. But for a long time I've been trying to figure out just what a racketeer is. I never went to school past the third grade but I graduated from ten universities of hard knocks and I have decided that a racketeer is a fellow who tries to get power, prestige or money.”

“Maybe I don't make it clear, but I figure that if I'm a racketeer, so are let's say editors. They'll print your articles in the hope of getting circulation from rival newspapers, for circulation means power, prestige and money. I'm circulation.”

... accused of operating an organisation to dodge taxes:

“As far as I'm concerned, it's the biggest fish story of all time.”

... on trial for tax evasion, advised by his attorney to wear a plain suit, rather than his normal expensive outfits:

“I'm sorry but I'd rather blow the goddamn case.”

... speaking to Newsweek magazine:

❛I'm like Coca-Cola. There are a lot of good drinks as good as Coca-Cola. Pepsi-Cola is a good drink. But Pepsi-Cola never got the advertising Coca-Cola got. I'm not Pepsi-Cola. I'm Coca-Cola because I got so much advertising.❜

... introduced by his mistress to a stock-broker who disapproved of her relationship with the Mafia boss:

❛We're in the same racket. We both gamble with other people's money.❜

Eddie Guerin, *infamous villain of the early century, asked to identify himself at the London Sessions:*

❛I'm Mr Smith of Nowhere.❜

Isaac Costner, *a defence witness in a Chicago kidnap trial, asked for his current occupation:*

❛I am a fugitive from justice.❜

Donald Hume, *who murdered Stanley Setty and threw his dismembered body out of a plane over the English Channel:*

❛I was wielding the dagger just like our Stone Age ancestors did 20,000 years ago.❜

Don Ciccio Coccia, *Sicilian godfather, concerned at the police presence as he welcomed Benito Mussolini to his hometown:*

❛Excellency, you're with me and you have nothing to worry about. Why do you need so many cops?❜

Roy Garner, *London villain, on being turned down for a firearms licence:*

❛This is not Sicily and I don't belong to the Mafia. I'm no gangster. If I am a murderer, robber and arsonist, what am I doing walking free?❜

Fred West:

‘I should go to hell, shouldn’t I, for what I’ve done?’

Thomas Campbell, *Glasgow villain, on his trial for the Ice-Cream War murders:*

‘There was a lot of lies told about me. They said I had a fleet of ice-cream vans – I had one. They painted me as some sort of Moriarty character. According to the papers, I was like a Mafia Don – nothing could happen in Carntyne without my say-so. It was a load of shite, that.’

Freddie Foreman, *on being charged with the murder of Frank ‘The Mad Axeman’ Mitchell:*

‘Prison officers at Leicester told me that if I was indeed guilty of the crime, I had performed a public service and should be awarded a medal the size of a dustbin lid.’

Howard Marks, *aka international cannabis dealer Mr Nice, recalling his first press interview:*

‘The article portrayed me as a nice, wicked stoner with brains and bottle.’

Dutch Schultz, *bootlegger and gangster, on why he adopted that name:*

‘It was short enough to fit the headlines. If I’d kept the name Flegenheimer, nobody would have heard of me.’

Moe Dalitz, *Mafia don, after being threatened in a restaurant by world heavyweight boxing champion, Sonny Liston:*

‘You’d better kill me, because if you don’t I’ll

make one telephone call and you'll be dead in twenty-four hours.'

John Gotti, *Mafia don, caught on police bugging equipment:*

'You tell this punk that me, John Gotti, will sever his fucking head off.'

Salvatore Giuliano, *Sicilian bandit on the run, in a note left under his plate at a Palermo restaurant, along with a large tip:*

'This is to show that Giuliano, the Champion of Sicily, can still come into Palermo whenever he likes.'

Frank Balistrieri, *Milwaukee mob leader, denying all allegations of extortion and racketeering:*

'The first time I heard the word Mafia was when I read it in the newspapers.'

Sam Giancana, *Mafia Godfather, on power:*

'Don't ever forget that I'm the "Justice of the Peace". If they do what I want, we'll take care of them. If they don't, well, we'll take care of that too.'

... asked by an army selection board in World War II for his profession:

'Me? I steal.' Sent home as a "constitutional psychopath", he later said, 'They thought I was crazy. I wasn't crazy, I was telling the truth.'

Tommaso Buscetta, *Sicilian "Godfather of Two Worlds" in a newspaper interview:*

'On my name weigh legends and fantasies, but also gross slanders. There is no proof of anything. I am a man like other men who hasn't done anything secret or mysterious to hide or defend. I have my loves, my life, my family and my children who are all in America. I'm not a mafioso. I have never been one and no one can prove anything against me.❜

... to newspaper reporters:

❛I am a mafioso; I have never done anything to apologise for.❜

... appealing against being extradited from Brazil:

❛The only gang I had in Brazil was my family.❜

Meyer Lansky, *Godfather of Godfathers, to the Kefauver inquiry into organised crime:*

❛I'm not one of those Jewish hotel owners in Miami Beach who tell you all sorts of stories just to please you. I will not allow you to persecute me because I'm a Jew.❜

James "Limey" Spenser, *Englishman who became a Chicago gangster in the 1920s:*

❛Something must be lacking in my moral make-up. When it comes to seeing things as "right" or "wrong", I am colour-blind.❜

John Dillinger, *America's "Public Enemy Number One", presenting a reporter with a "lucky" rabbit's foot:*

❛I shot him out of season. I guess I'm just a born criminal.❜

John McVicar, *in the 1960s Britain's "Most Wanted Man", now a respected writer on rock star, Roger Daltrey, who starred in the film of McVicar's escape from Durham Prison:*

❛How would you feel if the person playing you in a film does it better than you did in real life?❜

Tony Lambrianou, *on being a former associate of the Kray Twins:*

❛We're always made welcome wherever we go. I could open my own brewery with the amount of booze that comes at me. People keep on telling me what good things we did, the Robin Hood side of it. They always want to hear what I've got to say and they always tell me I didn't deserve the sentence I got, but Wendy keeps my feet on the ground. She'll say, "Tony, you've got red blood same as everybody else." ❜

Jeffrey Dahmer, *the Milwaukee Cannibal, on the comparison between his own life and that portrayed by Anthony Hopkins in "Silence of the Lambs":*

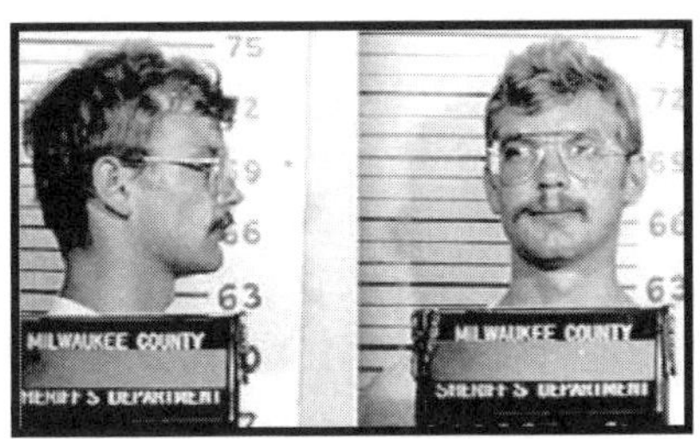

❛It's just a sick, pathetic, wretched, miserable life-story. That's all it is. How can it help anyone?❜

Ronnie Biggs, *fugitive Great Train Robber, writing in 1981:*

❛Why won't the British government show some compassion and understanding and allow me to lead a normal, hard-working life? Why do they persist in this charade which deprives me of the rights of an ordinary citizen? What are they trying to do? Make a criminal out of me?❜

Bugsy Goldstein, *New York hitman, to detectives:*

‘The papers say I’m Public Enemy Number 6. I should get a better spot. I’m working on it.’

John Wheater, *lawyer jailed for his part in the Great Train Robbery:*

‘I decided some time ago that I was not cut out to be a solicitor.’

Peter Scott, *former cat-burglar:*

‘I don’t think I was very greedy. I spent my life giving money to head waiters, tarts and the needy bookmakers. Of the two thieves on the cross with the Nazarene I rather see myself as the one who didn’t get into heaven.’

“College Harry”, *London villain of the pre-war period:*

‘Being a criminal, I have found, is – at least in one respect – akin to being a film or stage actor: the public tends to visualise the person concerned as having no existence outside his professional capacity.’

Martin Cahill, *‘The General’ of the Irish underworld, interviewed after emerging from a Dublin court in Micky Mouse boxer shorts:*

‘I will admit to nothing under the alias of The General, Micky Mouse or anyone else. If the gardai have evidence they should charge me. It’s all a game.’

Peppino Pes, *jailed Mafia hitman, asked by a visiting judge why he did not take advantage and eat better food in prison, since he controlled the canteen:*

‘Sir, I only do murders, I don’t steal meat!’

Johnny Torrio, *Al Capone's mentor, in an instruction that his minions obeyed all his life:*

‘No one is ever to mention my name. No one!’

Nathan Kaplan, *New York gangster, instructing his friends and family on the protocol of how to address him:*

‘Call me Jack the Dropper or Kid Dropper, that's all.’

Norman Selby, *alias Kid "The Real" McCoy, boxing champion and convicted killer:*

‘It's no fun telling people you're Kid McCoy if they've heard of you before.’

Edward Wilhelm Bentz, *American bank robber of the 1930s, who prided himself on his anonymity:*

‘I'm a big farmerish-looking sort of fellow, sort of easy-going, like to laugh and talk and be chummy with people, and that doesn't often match up with ideas about criminals. And I always liked nice things – went to good shows, stayed at good hotels, ate at the best places, and was always quiet and gentlemanly about it. People think crooks hide in cellars.’

Albert Spaggiari, *French master criminal:*

‘The only thing I have in common with the average citizen is a certain genetic similarity.’

David Stein, *the art forger who produced 400 fakes of modern masters, only 110 of which have so far been recognised:*

‘I can open an art catalogue anywhere in the world and recognise my stuff.’

Jacques Verges, *controversial French lawyer, responding on television to allegations that he was involved with his client, Carlos the Jackal, in terrorist activities:*

‘I admit everything and I’ll let you into a little secret. The assassination of the King of Yugoslavia, that was me...the Great Train Robbery, that was me too.’

Jamie Petrolini, *public school boy, convicted of a random killing in London:*

‘I am a chilled-out, mellow, friendly kid. OK? I’m into Indian music. I like things like the Levellers, Nirvana, Radiohead, stuff like that. I’m well into sports. I’m a bit of a Cat In The Hat. If you want a picture, get a drawing of a really cool teenager with hearts and peace and love and empathy all around the edge, because that is me.’

‘...Have you seen *My Own Private Idaho*? That was me when I got to Oxford...Have you seen *The Manchurian Candidate*, when the KGB hypnotised people and turned them into assassins and they haven’t a clue what’s going on? The same thing happened to me...I’m a bit of a hippy actually.’

The Duc du Praslin, *questioned after his wife was found murdered in her bedroom:*

‘I am a peer of France. I do not give explanations to police officers.’

Kenneth Erskine, *The Stockwell Strangler who murdered seven pensioners:*

‘I don’t remember killing anyone. I could have done it without knowing. I’m not sure if I did.’

Jackie Rosa, *London villain and disqualified driver, to police who found him dying in a car crash:*

‘It wasn't me who was driving.’

Takashi Sasakawa, *Japanese Yakusa boss, on the changing ways of crime:*

‘I am one of the last fools in this world.’

Martin Rivera Benitez, *Mexican hitman who took the heads of his victims to show his employers:*

‘I saw nothing wrong in killing for money. If I had not done it somebody else would.’

Marion Barry, *Mayor of Washington, to reporters as he was led off to jail after being convicted of cocaine charges:*

‘Got me set up! Ain't that a bitch!’

George Ince, *wrongly picked out in an identification parade as a murderer, asked to attend another parade to try to find the man who had slashed him with a razor during a prison football match:*

‘I wouldn't like to take the chance on identifying anyone. You know what I think of identification parades.’

Ian Brady, *Moors Murderer:*

‘I always liked the best seats in the cinema.’

The Life We Live

Paul Castellano, *Boss of Bosses, on Mafia ties:*

‘There are certain promises you make that are more sacred than anything that happens in a court of law, I don’t care how many Bibles you put your hand on. Some of the promises, it’s true, you make too young, before you really have an understanding of what they mean. But once you’ve made those first promises, other promises are called for. And the thing is, you can’t deny the new ones without betraying the old ones. The promises get bigger, there are more people to be hurt and disappointed if you don’t live up to them. Then, at some point, you’re called upon to make a promise to a dying man.’

Frank Coppola, *mafioso, asked by an Italian magistrate, ‘What is the Mafia?’:*

‘Your honour, there are three magistrates who would like to become procurators of the Republic. One is extremely intelligent, the second has the support of the government, and the third is an idiot, but he is the one who will get the job. That is the Mafia.’

Philip D'Andrea, *President of the Unione Siciliane, admitting that he had once heard of the Mafia when he was a child, asked by the Senate Crime Investigating Committee if it was a subject discussed among Italian families:*

“Oh, God, no. No sir! It's not discussed out of the home.”

Lucky Luciano, *on the Sicilian Mafia:*

“You might say it's like a private club that a lotta people belong to.”

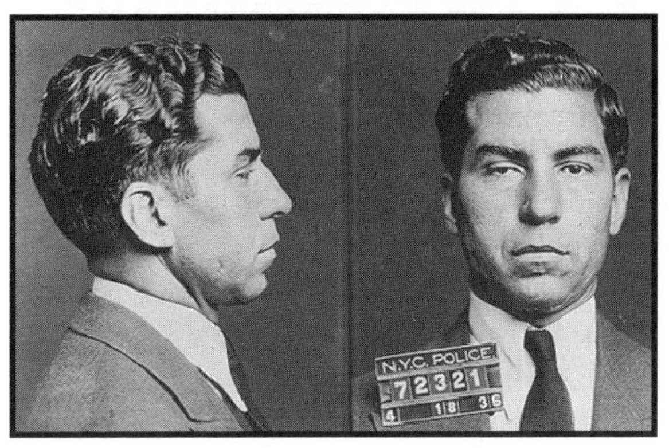

...looking back, in retirement:

“Killing? I hadda lifetime of it.”

John Gotti: *on the Mafia:*

“It's not a toy. I'm not in the mood for toys or games or kidding, no time. I'm not in the mood for clans. I'm not in the mood for gangs, I'm not in the mood for none of that stuff there. And this is gonna be a Cosa Nostra till I die. Be it an hour from now or be it tonight or be it a hundred years from now when I'm in jail. It's gonna be a Cosa Nostra.”

...showing irritation with the New York Mafia:

‘It’s this “thing of ours”. It’s gotten to be a circus. I’m not gonna leave a circus when I go to jail. I don’t wanna be a phoney.’

Joey Cantalupo, *Mafia man, on business:*

‘You get in all the legitimate businesses you can, make it legitimate, but you still have on the side all your illegal businesses still bringing in incomes. And it’s more and more money, more legitimate things and more illegal things. It’s just a vast, vast empire.’

Sammy ‘The Bull’ Gravano, *on the rules of the Mafia:*

‘We weren’t allowed to deal junk, we weren’t allowed to kill with bombs, we weren’t allowed to violate one another’s wives or kids, we weren’t allowed to raise our hands to one another, and they skipped by a few other rules.’

‘... When I was a kid I ran with gangs. I dropped out of school in the eighth grade. It didn’t seem wrong. It was the environment...The devil didn’t make me do it. I did it on my own.’

Heidi Fleiss, *Hollywood brothel-keeper who refused to name her clients:*

‘I’m tougher than Sammy the Bull. I kept my mouth shut.’

Sam Giancana, *Mafia Godfather, on the CIA:*

‘This coin shows one of the Roman Gods. This one has two faces, two sides. That’s what we are, the Outfit and the CIA, two sides of the same coin.’

Vincent Teresa, *American Mafia informer, on the difference between the old world and the new:*

‘These Sicilian mafiosi will run into a wall, put their head in a bucket of acid for you if they're told to, not because they're hungry but because they're disciplined. They've been brought up from birth over there to show respect and honour, and that's what these punks over here don't have. Once they're told to get someone, that person hasn't a chance. They'll get him if they have to bust into his house in the middle of the night, shoot him, bite him, eat him, suck the blood out of his throat. They'll get him because they were told to do it.’

‘... Sometimes you have to do things you don't like. Sometimes people who were real close to you have to be put to sleep. I went to so many goddamn funerals of guys who were like brothers to me, I can't count them. The old guys stand there at the funeral with stone faces, and they go over to the widow and say “Gee...it's rough... I'm sorry” when it was them that put the husband away!’

Jim Harter, FBI agent, *on the difference between a Mafia and a Yardie contract murder:*

‘When the Mob wants to hit you, they just get you and they do it very cleanly. They're professionals. This group, the posses, makes big messes because they don't give a damn about anybody. They are going to take you out the first chance they get – whatever the circumstances.’

Pittsburgh Phil Strauss of Murder Inc., *on a job well done:*

‘It was an easy pop. I take the ax and sink it in the guy’s head. It’s the kind of thing that will make a lot of holler. Dames and guys will make a run out of there. I just run with them – and the getaway is a cinch. This is a natural.’

Frank Costello, *Mafia boss, speaking to reporter in later life:*

‘All I know I stole. If I saw you hold a cigarette a certain way, and I liked it, I would steal it from you.’

Lou Eppolito, *New York police officer:*

‘There’s an expression in organised crime, it’s called cleaning house. If you whack somebody, then you have to whack everybody who’s going to cause you any trouble for whacking the first guy.’

Giovanni Falcone, *Italian anti-Mafia investigator:*

‘Becoming part of the Mafia is the equivalent of a religious conversion. One cannot retire from the priesthood...or the Mafia.’

‘...The culture of death does not belong solely to the Mafia; all of Sicily is impregnated with it. Here the day of the dead is a huge celebration.’

Yakusa boss of the Sumiyoshi syndicate, *explaining the difference between the Japanese and American mafias:*

‘In the winter we give the sunny half of the street to the common people because we survive on their work. In the summer, we Yakusa walk on the sunny side, to give them the cool, shaded half.’

Gaetano Badalementi *at the Pizza Connection trial, recalling the ease with which mafiosi could obtain false passports:*

‘We used to buy them like other people buy shirts.’

Charles Carboni, *French lawyer, on the Corsican vendetta, which lasted for over a decade:*

‘In my view the vendetta is a primitive form of justice. The Corsican bandit who kills an adversary to avenge one of his relatives is convinced that what he does is just. In his own mind, paradoxical as it may seem, he is not a wrongdoer. He kills his enemies in cold blood, but he would not harm a fly.’

J. Edgar Hoover, *head of the FBI:*

‘A criminal does not look upon himself as such. You must accept this as an axiom if you ever are to learn the slightest rules about protecting yourself, your home and your family. His viewpoint is this: he wants something. That is the end of the matter. Wanting it, he feels he should have it. No ideas of justice ever enter his mind; if they do, they are quickly swamped by selfishness. The old excuse of “I did not stop to think” was never true, although this alibi for crime has worked to the amelioration of sentences until it is threadbare. The true statement, which is rarely voiced, is: “I did not stop to think of anyone but myself.”’

Jimmy Boyle, *Scottish villain-turned-writer:*

‘The “criminal code” isn’t a thing that has been written up by top gangsters. It is an unwritten code of ethics. There are done things and things that are not done. It isn't the "done" thing to grass or inform on anyone. It isn't the "done" thing to bump or cheat someone from a robbery that you've all taken part in. There are lots of these unwritten rules that could fill another book but these are just two examples that exist between guys in crime and on the whole they abide by them.❜

Patrick Meehan, *former Glasgow safecracker:*
❛To become a good villain – an earner – takes as much thought, as much preparation, as much skill and a good deal more nerve than anything in straight society. The risks, the satisfaction of the rebellion against authority, are as big a reward as the cash.❜

Glasgow detective, *on gang members, known as "Neds":*
❛Neds have one characteristic in common: a tendency to engage is senseless argument which not infrequently ends in violence.❜

Jim Phelan, *convict-turned-writer:*
❛The underworld is not a place – one may meet its personnel anywhere. "Respectable" writers have to tell a whacking lie about this, to start with. They have to pretend that all underworld people live in slums, have bristly chins, drop their aitches and carry a mask and jemmy wherever they go. From Fleet Street to Hollywood the poor devils pitch that puerile falsehood – for money.❜

Dave Courtney, *London TV-crook-turned-author, on villainy:*
❛Real villains call it "work". As in, as an armed

robber would say, I went out on a bit of work the other day. He wouldn't say "I'm just going out into the underworld to meet some other villains to rob a bank, babe. Pie and mash for tea, is it?"'

James Saunders, *London solicitor, in the late 1980s:*

'At any one time there are about two hundred heavy-duty professional criminals in London. They go round about ten or fifteen clubs massaging each others' egos by the conventional process of flattery or the less conventional process of shooting at each other. Some make some money and have a good time for quite a short period of time; most don't. To call them mugs would not be very fair but they are not the people who make the money. What are the criteria of success? We quite often deal with people who are fingered for this, that or the other and as soon as the shout goes up they're over in Spain or Costa Rica or Brazil or wherever it may be. Almost invariably, within a comparatively short period of time, they come back to England. They don't need to for any objective reason but they can't live without the smell of drains, fish and chips and the taste of Watney's. These are the people for whom success is when they walk into a club everyone stands to one side, flatters them and allows them to buy a drink for everyone. Undoubtedly that is one of the major reasons for them to do what they do.'

Leslie Payne, *former business adviser to the Kray Twins:*

'Aristocrats and successful businessmen have a great deal in common: boredom and selfishness, ample money and free time and a complete lack of interest in conventional, cautious, bourgeois morality. The fallen professional man, the struck-off barrister, the crooked accountant falls naturally into company with them.’

Tommy Wisbey, *Great Train Robber:*

‘There’s no such a thing as the underworld. They’re just criminals aren’t they, known criminals.’

Mark Benney, *on the criminal classes:*

‘The wide people are totally indifferent to the virtues defined and possessed by the mug-majority. They live gaily, love promiscuously, drink vastly, sing loudly, lie brazenly, swagger outrageously and hate dangerously. Above all they never work.’

Edward Bunker, *Mr Blue in Reservoir Dogs:*

‘Most thieves steal or rob only when poverty is fast approaching or is already at hand. I tried to avoid that mistake. When I was a thief it was a profession practised twenty four hours a day.’

Chopper Read, *Australian hoodlum whose life was celebrated in a box office hit movie:*

‘If you’re going to enter the criminal world, what’s the use just finishing up a name on a tombstone and no one has ever heard of you? Bugger that. You go all the way or not at all.’

Donald ‘Tony the Greek’ Frankos, *hitman-cum-informer, recalling an earlier period of his criminal life:*

‘I didn’t want to go straight. No boring sessions

with do-gooder social workers for this cookie. No bullshit therapy from a shrink who would say I hated my uncle. Forget denial and struggling to make ends meet on some begged-for, dead-end job. "You're a criminal pure and simple" I told myself, "so go for it whole hog."'

John McVicar:

'The professional thief leads a difficult and hazardous life, which only the foolish and optimistic or the patient and cunning believe they can survive.'

Mikhail Dyomin, *thief-turned-poet, on his homeland:*

'The legitimate world bears the same relationship to a Russian thief as a henhouse to a fox. The problems of the henhouse are of no interest to the fox. His only concern is to penetrate it, satisfy his appetite and get the hell out.'

George Smithson, *country-house burglar of the 1920s:*

'The ordinary crook too often shows his hand by parading his cash and new clothes. It is one of the failings of crookdom to like to be flashy and attract attention.'

Eddie Guerin, *turn-of-the-century bank robber, nfamous in Britain, America and France:*

'Dissect the psychology of the average criminal and you will find there is little in him but a blind intuition to get the necessities of life with the least possible trouble. He doesn't really think of what he is doing – or he wouldn't do it. I can claim – for what it is worth – acquaintance with all the famous crooks of England and America. Some of them are men who have made a lot of money in their time, but they all always a robber. Being a thief isn't a permanent condition with me. It isn't something unchangeable like the colour of your eyes or your pubic hair. I'm only a robber when I'm in peak form or in the depths of despair. Stealing is a noble profession.'

Valerio Viccei, *on the motivation that led him to rob £60 million from the Knightsbridge Safe Deposit Co. in London:*

'Crime had become to me what narcotics are to a junkie: I simply could not live without it. Like heavy drugs, crime at its highest level generates the worst kind of addiction.'

'...In over twenty years I had never compromised on anything. I had always been my own man and chosen whichever accomplice or target I thought fit. I was the planner and the leader in the field as well; I always took the major risks and never tried to hide from the responsibilities that my rank implied. I was always the first to go in and the last to leave and that is the only way to command respect and loyalty.'

Joseph "Yellow Kid" Weil, *highly successful con man in his day, asked at the age of a hundred if he were able to get out of his wheelchair and go on the streets, would he still try to con people:*

'Does a hungry dog like food?'

...talking to crime writer J.R.Nash about his criminal activities:

'I never could resist taking a sucker. Never. I had to scratch that itch.'

Alvin "Old Creepy" Karpis, *who spent more time in Alcatraz than any other convict:*

❛My profession was robbing banks, knocking off payrolls and kidnapping rich men. I was good at it.❜

Harry Pierpont *of the Dillinger Gang:*

❛My conscience doesn't hurt me. I stole from the bankers. They stole from the people. All we did was help raise the insurance rates.❜

Spike O'Donnell, *Chicago bootlegger:*

❛Life with me is just one bullet after another. I've been shot at and missed so often, I've a notion to hire out as a professional target.❜

Jack Black, *American criminal of the early 1900s:*

❛I learned the lesson of violence in prison, and I believed that I lived in a world of violence, had to use violence and use it first. I had no more thought of right or wrong than a wolf that prowls the prairie. I had formed the criminal habit. Habit is the strongest thing in life and criminals obey the impulse to commit a crime almost subconsciously.❜

Harry Vickers, *widely known in the 1930s as "Flannel Foot", on his life of burglary:*

❛The hours suited me.❜

Ruby Sparks, *London smash-and-grab robber, on his lifestyle in the late 1920s:*

❛Why? You may ask. Why did we have to keep grafting, with all the loot we'd had off? I'd nicked stuff valued a quarter of a million pounds in three or four years. We'd split between us over £50,000 cash from the buyers we'd sold it to – where was all that money gone? I couldn't properly tell you. It gets knocked out in night clubs and bars, buying drinks for hangers-on, and playing Big Head. You go gambling in stuffy little spielers, I mean gambling dens. It isn't so much you try to lose it, but you got it so easily that you don't really care. You walk into a bar where the fraternity assemble and the glad shouts of welcome go up. "Aye, aye, it's the famous Ruby Sparks!" Old lags who are on the ribs touch you for a fifty, brassy little tarts pout at you and wheedle a five or ten, and two hours drinking and showing off can cost you easily £300. You buy a pair of socks and because the shopman talks with a posh accent and you can't, you buy revenge by handing him a five for the pair of socks and saying "Keep the change, son." ❜

... on spending:

❛It probably sounds a bit milky if I was to say now that the reason which makes thieves and villains get through their ill-gotten wages so sharpish is they must inside themselves feel somehow guilty about it, but there's got to be some explanation why why we all raced the gelt like we did.❜

Joe Cannon, *London villain:*

❛I've come to the conclusion that I was simply born rotten, just as surely as if I'd been given a stocking mask and a sawn-off shotgun as christening presents.❜

Bertie Smalls, *armed robber and the first supergrass:*

‘This nervous tension I used to feel before a job didn’t stay with me all the time, only till I got started. Once I start I feel completely calm, one hundred per cent, everything comes brilliant to me...I might be fogged up a minute or two before but the minute it’s on it’s like the sun coming out from behind a cloud.’

Mehmet Ali Agca, *who tried to kill Pope John Paul II in 1981, on his all-consuming enthusiasm for terrorism:*

‘I make no distinction between Fascist and Communist terrorists. My terrorism is not red or black – it is red and black.’

Timothy McVeigh, *the Oklahoma City bomber who killed 168 people and wounded 600:*

‘If Government is the teacher, violence would be an acceptable option. What did we do to Sudan? What did we do to Afghanistan? Belgrade? What are we doing with the death penalty? It appears they use violence as an option all the time.’

Wise Words

Bruce Reynolds, *mastermind of the Great Train Robbery:*

‘Clever criminals don't get caught.’

John Gotti, *while being secretly taped by police:*

‘This is how we get in trouble, we talk.’

Clyde Barrow, *of Bonnie & Clyde fame:*

‘It's easier to run than explain.’

Ma Barker, *matriarch of the notorious Barker Family:*

‘Crime does pay – if you're careful.’

Thomas Campbell, *convicted of the Glasgow Ice-Cream War murders, on his upbringing in crime:*

‘If you're involved with head cases, the best way to survive is to become the best of the head cases.’

Don Vito Cascioferro, *Sicily's first Mafia overlord, on how to apply extortion but not bankrupt the victim:*

‘You have to skim the cream off the milk without breaking the bottle.’

Joseph 'Yellow Kid' Weil, *American con-man, explaining how he was able to swindle gullible victims out of $8 million in a forty year career:*

‘The average person is ninety-nine per cent animal

and one per cent human. The ninety-nine per cent that is animal causes very little trouble. But the one per cent that is human causes all our woes.’

Willie Sutton, *bank robber, described by a prosecutor:*

‘He isn’t a Robin Hood, he’s just a hood.’

Theodore Allen, *self-proclaimed wickedest man in New York:*

‘Right is when you get away with it. Wrong is when you are caught.’

Judge Taylor, *in the trial of New York crime boss, Louis “Lepke” Buchalter, betrayed by an informer:*

‘When rogues fall out, it is a wise man’s delight.’

Giuseppe Genco Russo, *Sicilian godfather, on the US Mafia’s internal disputes over the heroin trade:*

‘Blessed is he who is far away when a hundred dogs fight over a bone.’

Edward Bunker, *convict-turned-writer who played Mr Blue in Reservoir Dogs:*

‘London has apparently the highest fist-fight rates in the world. It’s good if you weigh 230lbs like me but if I weighed 110 I’d rather have a gun.’

... on firearms:

‘There are 200 million of them in the U.S. My attitude is I wish nobody had them, nobody, but I’m not giving mine up till they’re down to at least 50 million. When they get down to that, I’ll give mine up. The cops don’t want anybody to have guns except them – I wonder why?’

Horatio Bottomley, *crooked MP, later jailed for seven years:*

'Past histories, earthly lapses, blotted pages in the book of life – well, what of them? Let him that is without sin cast the first stone! And remember that, whatever his faults, each man has been given the opportunity of supreme attainment.'

Razor Smith, *serving eight life sentences for armed robbery:*

'By law I have to declare my previous convictions to any prospective employer so I might as well turn up for job interviews dressed as the Grim Reaper and sucking on a crack pipe. No one in their right mind is going to employ me.'

Frederick Kernochan, *New York judge, to a Senate committee investigating rackets in 1933:*

'Racketeering is a new word. But what they do is old.'

Michael Chirtoff, *whose prosecution of mobsters Louis Manna, Martin Cassella and Richard DeSciscio resulted in sentences of 80 years, 80 years and 75 years:*

'They are going to spend the rest of their lives in prison – unless they live a very long time.'

Kakuji Inagawa, *Japanese gangster, giving advice to his Yakusa members:*

'Beware of the weak, for the strong will take care of themselves.'

Nikolaus Chrastny, *robber, drug dealer and escaper, on how as a boy he was expelled from a Catholic college for casting doubt on the Bible:*

'I asked how Noah was able, in the Palestine desert, to take a penguin on board the Ark.'

Roger Benton, *forger, on the necessity for a criminal to keep on the move:*

'A rambling forger gathers no handcuffs.'

Scotland Yard detective, *on Yardie violence:*

'They have a philosophy that it is a short life but a sweet one.'

Valerio Viccei, *who, in 1987, committed Britain's biggest ever armed robbery, offering advice to Chancellor of the Exchequer, Norman Lamont:*

'I could give Mr Lamont a few financial tips. I know a lot about banks – I've been into many in my time.'

...sentenced to 22 years imprisonment:

'The law should not be afflictive, but educational and without vengeance. The criminal is an erring son of society, but always one of its creatures.'

Arnold Rothstein, *the 'Mr Big' of New York in the 1920s, instructing staff who worked in his clubs and brothels:*

'Treat the sucker right. He is paying your salary. His stupidity is our income. You must never insult him, just cheat him with a smile.'

Carlos Lehder, *Columbian drug baron:*

'Marijuana is for the people. Cocaine is for milking the rich.'

Nick 'Crow' Caramadi, *Mafia racketeer, on victims' greed:*

'You show me a guy that's greedy and I'll rob him. No matter how, I'll find a way to rob him. Because if he's got greed in him there's always a way. Just find the thing that he likes the most. When a guy is greedy, you could make him believe blue is white. You could make him believe orange is black. I mean, this is what kind of suckers there are.’

...after turning informer:

‘The Mafia. What is it? It’s a brotherhood of evil.’

... asked how he acquired the nickname “Crow”:

‘A crow is a shrewd bird.’

Howard Marks, *Oxford scholar-turned international cannabis smuggler on politicians’ attitude to drugs:*

‘There are four ways of distributing them – medical prescription, licence, supermarket and organised crime. Why they choose the latter I don’t know.’

Dutch Schultz, *asked in the 1930s why a man of his wealth did not wear tailor-made suits and silk shirts:*

‘Such displays are vulgar. Personally I think only queers wear silk shirts – I never bought one in my life.’

Joe Adonis, *New York gangster, described at his death by a detective:*

‘The millions Joe A. took out of the county didn’t do him a damn bit of good in the end. He waded through blood to get it and he croaked with empty pockets in a dirty shack.’

Tom Keating, *art faker who fooled the experts:*

‘I have enough work to make me rich beyond my wildest dreams. But I’ve met many millionaires and they’ve all been miserable.’

Helen James, *who, concerned that the relatives of her husband Robert had a tendency to die after he insured them, refused his request to take out a policy on her life:*

'People who have insurance always die of something strange.'

Johnny Spanish, *lone-wolf protection racketeer in early 1990s New York, to a gambling den owner who asked why he should have to hand over half his takings:*

'Because if youse don't I'll bump youse off and take it all.'

Louis Piquett, *Indiana lawyer, replying to a friend who warned that he should not handle hoodlum clients:*

'They're the only ones who have money these days.'

Richard 'Dixie' Davis, *lawyer to Arthur Flegenheimer, better known as Dutch Schultz:*

'You can insult Arthur's girl, spit in his face, push him around – and he'll laugh. But don't steal a dollar from his accounts. If you do, you're dead.'

Angelo Bruno*'s advice to his daughter:*

'Anybody who makes money illegally these days must be crazy. There are so many opportunities to make money the right way.'

Florida state attorney, *speaking of* **Ted Bundy**, *murderer of twenty-three women:*

'People think a criminal is a hunchbacked, cross-eyed little monster, slithering through the dark, leaving a trail of slime. They're human beings.'

Ted Bundy, *questioned about his crimes:*

❛I may not have all the answers, but I have all the ones which count.❜

Kakuji Inagawa, *Japan's most powerful godfather of the post-war years, on Yakusa public relations:*

❛I like casual conversations but it's difficult to do interviews. I don't want to become a showpiece. We're part of society's hidden world and not meant to be more.❜

Mehmet Ali Agca, *who attempted to assassinate Pope John Paul II in St Peter's Square, Rome:*

❛It's easy to be a terrorist in Italy.❜

Charles Bronson, *formerly Michael Peterson, reputedly Britain's most disruptive prisoner:*

❛Insanity drove me mad.❜

Angelo De Carlo, *sixty seven year old Mafia boss, on his way to prison:*

❛I've got to die sometime, so I might as well go this way.❜

F. Lee Bailey, *lawyer, on the iniquities of the U.S. legal system:*

❛The system is screwed up from indictment on. To start with, there is nothing less grand than a grand jury. The typical grand jury is a flock of sheep led by the prosecutor across the meadow to the finding he wants. Then, if he finds it politically expedient, he can always say, "Hell, don't blame me; the grand jury got the indictment." Meanwhile the target of all the potshotting learns that although the state didn't come around to ask if he was having tea with the Pope on the day in question (this is considered a fair alibi in legal circles), he's just been accused of knocking off his business partner...’

William Bentley, *father of Derek Bentley, dubiously convicted of the murder of a policeman and hanged in 1953:*

‘The law is a machine that grinds out life and death and good and ill. It has no heart.’

Adolf Hofrichter, *who denied the murder of a fellow officer in the Austrian army:*

‘A murder is a crime that is often punishable by death. Why then is the butcher not killed?’

Danny Ahearn, *New York gangster:*

‘The best way to kill a man is not to confide in anybody.’

David Berkowitz, *the serial killer, "Son of Sam":*

‘There will always be killers because any individual with death and destruction on his mind will always be guaranteed plenty of publicity and a willing audience when he turns to anti-social acts for recognition or whatever else.’

Brian Lane, *defending his encyclopaedia of serial killers:*

‘If someone is evil they will do evil things. If you go out and kill tomorrow and they find my encyclopedia and a copy of Bambi in your bedroom, who is to say which drove you to murder? There have been plenty of books on the Second World War but they have not created a third one, have they?’

Pittsburgh Phil Strauss, *Murder Inc. hitman:*

‘It's okay to do a murder – if I'm not caught.’

...described by a police commissioner in 1934:

‘This man is a paid assassin. When you meet such men, draw quickly and shoot accurately.’

Bugsy Siegel, *assuring a frightened contractor building his Flamingo Hotel and Casino in Las Vegas that he need not fear the Syndicate:*

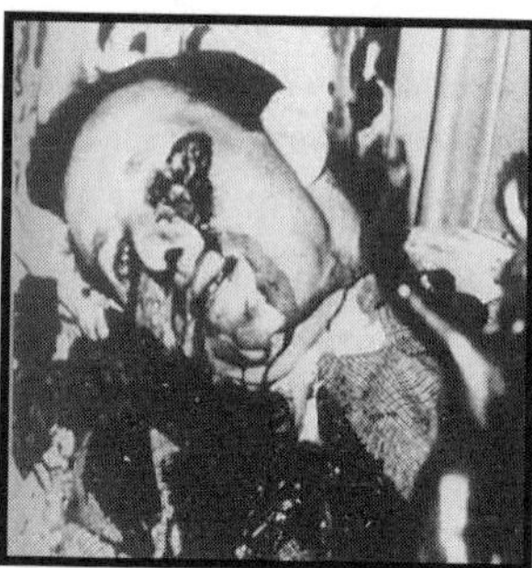

Bugsy Seigel was killed in 1947 in a Beverley Hills mansion with a .30 carbine rifle on the orders of Lucky Luciano and Meyer Lansky

‘We only kill each other.’

Junior Blair, *contract killer, as he waited to die on Missouri's Death Row:*

‘Death is certain – life is not.’

Vinenzo Napoli, *Mafia arms dealer, unwittingly advising an undercover FBI agent:*

‘The best one for a hit is a .22. It's nice, it's quiet, it don't make problems.’

Robert Fabian – *'Fabian of the Yard' – on gunmen:*

‘Unless he is insane, the brown-eyed criminal does not carry a gun with intent to use it. He may think he does but the showdown proves him wrong. The man who shoots to kill has grey eyes.’

Sir Hartley Shawcross, *at the trial of John George Haigh, the Acid Bath Killer:*

‘There is no such thing as a nice murder.’

Waxey Gordon, *1920s bootlegger, to Joe "The Greaser" Rosenzweig, who had informed on him:*

‘You used to be my boss, so I won't kill you now. I'm gonna give you enough scratch to take a powder. But if me or any of my boys ever see you in New York again, you're gonna be pushing up lilacs in a cemetery and you'll go into a box with pennies on your eyelids.’

Albert De Salvo, *the Boston Strangler, on his crimes:*

‘Perhaps the doctors can cut out the corner of my brain that made me do those things.’

Dr Marcel Petiot, *who claimed that his twenty-four wartime murders were committed in in the name of patriotism:*

‘When one sets out on a voyage one takes all one's luggage with one.’

John Dillinger, *protesting to police that he did not need to be handcuffed to a post behind the pilot's seat as he was about to be flown back to Indiana:*

‘Hell, I don't jump out of these things.’

Giuseppe Zangara, *would-be assassin of President Franklin D. Roosevelt, as he fired shots which missed, fatally striking the Mayor of Chicago:*

‘There are too many people starving to death!’

Dave Berman, *unconcerned at being charged with the kidnap of a New York bootlegger:*

‘Hell, the worst I can get is life.’

A neighbour of Howard Unruh, *who massacred thirteen people in one day in 1949:*

‘He was a quiet one, that guy. He was all the time figuring to do this thing. You gotta watch them quiet ones.’

Albert Spaggiari:

‘I'm not out to reform the world. It is what it is. I've never been corrupt enough to face the world with luck on my side.’

Angelo DeCarlo, *explaining his popularity in the New Jersey underworld:*

‘All these other racket guys who get a few bucks want to become legitimate!’

Mark David Chapman, *killer of John Lennon:*

‘I remember, even when I was very young, something that my mother told me – “Mark, you don't wear well with people.”’

John Gotti, *to henchman, Frank Locascio:*

‘We are where we belong. We're in the positions we belong in Frankie and nobody could change that. But this business thing. Ahh, it's brothers! Please. And if you robbing people on my behalf, stop When I say “robbing,” I don't mean robbing. You know, ya taking work out of other people's mouths You wanna rob people on my behalf, stop on my behalf.’

Donald ‘Tony the Greek’ Frankos:

‘I recommend violence to anyone unfortunate enough to end up in prison. Usually if an inmate fights back the first time – say he cuts his attacker with a razor – he has a good chance of being left alone. Prison predators reason that there are too many easy marks, so why harass someone nutty enough to fight back.❜

Eddie Bentz, *bookish bank robber and pioneer in the art of "casing" jobs, on the difference between himself and other criminals:*

❛Books are what did it. A lot of those mugs never had been in a public library. It pays to be educated.❜

Frank Costello, *Mafia boss, to film actor Anthony Quinn:*

❛You know, kid, where I come from – you shake hands, you keep your word. If you don't, send back the hand.❜

...asked by Senator Estes Kefauver how he could curb gambling in the United States

❛Burn the stables and shoot the horses.❜

...to reporters, after being convicted of tax evasion and sentenced to five years jail:

❛I want to give you fellows some advice. Remember this – when you spend money, spend cash and don't have any checks. If your wife has any money, have her declare it right away, or they will be after you.❜

The Begum Aga Khan, *witness at the Aix-en-Provence trial of robbers who had stolen her jewels in 1949, asked by one of the defendants' lawyers if she thought his client had been menacing:*

❛No, but he had a machine-gun. I would have preferred him to be menacing and not to have the gun pointing at me.❜

Mad Frankie Fraser, *London villain:*

❛I was certified insane in the army during the war, when I was discharged. Then I was certified in 1947 at Wandsworth Prison – when I acted mad. I was only doing two years and I'd lost all my remission and this guy called Charlie Walters – I'll never forget his name – he told me how good it was...I said "Are you sure Charlie?" He said "Stand on me Frank."❜

Meyer Lansky, *Godfather of Godfathers, "Chairman of the Board" of the National Crime Syndicate, to Frank Costello who was concerned about his own and his friends' poor reputations:*

❛Don't worry, don't worry. Look at history. Look at the Astors and the Vandebilts, all those big society people. They were the worst thieves – and now look at them. It's just a matter of time.❜

...explaining why he was reading a history book, a grammar book and a book of French quotations – all at the same time:

❛These are the things you need with no education, because you can get mixed up.❜

...on the Mafia:

❛We're bigger than US steel.❜

... advising Paul 'The Waiter' Ricca, later to become Boss of Bosses in Chicago:

❛We'll make you rich. Play the waiting game, keep your name out of the newspapers and build your own organisation.❜

Tommaso Buscetta, *Sicilian supergrass, to Giovanne Falcone, investigator who was later murdered by the Mafia:*

❛First they'll try to kill me, then it will be your turn.' And they won't give up until they succeed.❜

Murray 'The Camel' Humphreys, *advising an associate to remain living in the city:*

‘Smart money doesn't go to the suburbs. You and your family will stick out like a sore thumb and the feds will always know exactly where you are. Bad idea Tony.’

Christopher Craig, *convicted with Bentley of the murder of PC Miles in 1952:*

‘What I've never been able to understand is how I shot him between the eyes when he was facing away from me and was going the wrong way.’

Nicky Arnstein, *concerned about his friend Arnold Rothstein's habit of constantly doing numerical tricks and mental arithmetic exercises:*

‘It just isn't good for you A.R. It isn't normal and you'll hurt your brain.’

Reverend John Schmitt *in a sermon, referring to Ed Gein – grave robber, killer of women and inspiration for the novel and movie, Psycho:*

‘We're all human and make mistakes. We could have made the same mistakes.’

Henry Lee Lucas, *serial killer, thirteen years and around two hundred victims after he warned prison authorities that he should not be released from an earlier jail sentence:*

‘I told them before I ever left prison that I was going to commit crimes, told them the type of crimes I was going to commit, and they wouldn't believe it. They said I was going regardless of whether I liked it or not. And the day I got out of jail is the day I started killing.’

Joseph 'Yellow Kid' Weil, *American con man who disliked the use of weapons:*

‘I'm telling you, we've got to clean house. Got to throw out these people who are ruining our profession!’

Michael Kitto, *on being sentenced to life imprisonment on his fortieth birthday in the "Monster Butler" murder case:*

‘Life begins at 40!’

Al Capone, *from his prison cell in Alcatraz:*

‘Bolshevism is knocking at our gates. We can't afford to let it in. We have got to organise ourselves against it and put our shoulders together and hold fast. We must keep America whole and safe and unspoiled. We must keep the workers away from Red literature and Red ruses. We must see that his mind remains healthy.’

‘....I'll have to hand it to Napoleon as the world's greatest racketeer, but I could have wised him up on some things. The trouble with that guy was he got the swelled head. He overplayed his hand and they made a bum out of him. He should have had sense enough after that Elba jolt to kiss himself out of the game. But he was just like the rest of us. He didn't know when to quit and had to get back in the racket. He simply put himself on the spot. That made it easy for the other gangs to take him and they were no dumbbells. If he had lived in Chicago it would have been a sawed-off shotgun Waterloo for him. He didn't wind up in a ditch as a coroner's case but they took him for a one-way ride to St Helena, which was about as tough a break.'

Warden Johnson of Alcatraz, *hearing on the radio that Al Capone regularly ordered silk underwear from a London haberdasher:*

'That's funny. I just left Capone and I distinctly remember he was wearing regulation long johns because they were held up with a safety pin.'

Dion O' Bannion, *to the brother of Davy "Yiddles" Miller, whom he had shot during the interval at a theatre:*

'You're a lucky lad. Now go pick up Yiddles and take him to a doctor and tell him to keep his mouth shut in the future.'

Horation Bottomley, *crooked MP, under cross-examination at a bankruptcy hearing, asked why he had earlier said that he did not keep race-horses:*

'I gave you a correct answer. I never kept race-horses. They keep me.'

Jack Leach, *old-time jockey, warning racegoers against placing bets with welshers:*

'Never bet with a bookmaker if you see him knocking spikes in his shoes.'

Jack Spot, *London gangster of the 1950s:*

'Hit 'em hard enough and they won't come back for more.'

Joe Adonis, *mafioso, asked by the Kefauver Committee on Organised Crime why he had moved from Brooklyn to New Jersey:*

'I like the climate there better.'

Charlie Peace, *Victorian burglar and murderer, on singing hymns:*

‘Makes a man feel nearer ’is Maker,
to sing them lovely tunes.’

...in a chance meeting with the public hangman, William Marwood, who some years later would hang him:

‘If ever you have to do the job for me, be sure you grease the rope well to let me slip.’

Arthur Calvert, *to his wife Louie, who had just been sentenced to death for murder:*

‘Well lass, it can’t be helped.’

Phil Kaufman, *on his former jail-mate, Charles Manson:*

‘There are a lot of people around Los Angeles who still believe in Charlie. Every once in a while you read about people who are Manson followers. Charlie talked apples when you talked pears.’

Sam Giancana, *suffering harassmant by police surveillance, to an associate who insisted on enthusing about ancient ruins he had seen in Greece:*

‘Ruins? I got coppers coming out of my eyeballs and you sit there telling me about ruins! Listen to me, Phil, listen real good! Ruins ain’t garbage! Forget about them goddamn ruins!’

Machine-Gun Jack McGurn: *Written on a card found in his left hand after he was gunned down in a Chicago bowling alley:*

‘You’ve lost your job,
You’ve lost your dough,
Your jewels and handsome houses.
But things could be worse, you know.
You haven’t lost your trousers.’

Stephen Andretta, *who went to jail for contempt, rather than give evidence in the Jimmy Hoffa murder case:*

‘They spent ten million dollars trying to throw Hoffa in jail, and now they’ve spent a figure very close to it trying to find out what happened to him.’

Mean Words

John Dillinger, *telephoning Captain Matt Leach, head of Indiana State Police, under whose nose he had raided two police stations and robbed a bank of $74,000:*

‘This is John Dillinger. How are you, you stuttering bastard?’

Joseph ‘Yellow Kid’ Weil, *swindler:*

‘Lies were the foundation of my schemes. A lie is an allurement, a fabrication that can be embellished into a fantasy. Truth is cold, sober fact, not so comfortable to absorb. A lie is more palatable. The most detested person in the world is the one who always tells the truth.’

...speaking of the victims whom he tricked out of $8million in a 35 year career:

‘They may have been respectable, but they were never any good. They wanted something for nothing. I gave them nothing for nothing.’

Big Bill Thompson, *Mayor of Chicago, blaming King George V of England for prohibition:*

‘I shouldn’t be surprised if the King had something to do with slipping over the Volstead Act on us so all their distillers can make fortunes selling us bootleg. If George comes to Chicago I’ll punch him in the snoot.’

Crazy Joe Gallo, *to an extortion victim who asked if he could have time to think over the offer of protection:*

‘Sure, you can have three months in the hospital, on me.’

Dutch Schultz, *on restaurants:*

‘These places need protection. There's hundreds of them in New York alone. A stink bomb in the rush hour or a worm in a batch of bread dough...anything could ruin a restaurant.’

Santo Grasso, *an Italian living in France, who murdered his next door neighbours:*

‘They were too noisy. I couldn't sleep. It was Sunday.’

Keith Eugene Wells, *who clubbed two strangers to death in a bar in Idaho:*

‘I was a predator on the prowl for prey.’

Thomas Ross Young, *Glasgow murderer, to police wishing to interview him about other cases:*

‘My initials are T.RY. If you want to know about other murders – try and try again.’

George Woolfe, *in a note to his girlfriend, before murdering her:*

‘I've made the acquaintance of a young lady I admire much better than you, therefore you had better do the same and think no more of me. PS I am indeed thankful I have got rid of you easily.’

Steven Judy, *rapist and murderer, to the jury trying him:*

‘You'd better put me to death. Because next time it might be one of you or your daughter.’

Carmine Galante, *the capo di tutti capo of Mafia Row, Lewisburg Penitentiary, expressing animosity towards a rival:*

‘When I get out I’ll make Carlo Gambino shit in the middle of Times Square.’

Roy di Meo, *captain in the Gambino family, impatient at the length of time his men were taking to chop up the corpse of a murder contract victim:*

‘Listen, I’ll cut – you wrap.’

Donald ‘Tony the Greek’ Frankos:

‘Most gangsters have just one solution for a problem. Kill it.’

Philip Leonetti, *Mafia underboss-turned informer, on his uncle, Mafia boss Nick Scarfo:*

‘He always wanted the reputation...he always said like Paul Muni said in that movie, *Scarface*, he said, “You gotta use this machine gun, you gotta kill people and you gotta keep on killin’ ’em to be the boss...You just can’t stop, you gotta keep killin ’em.”’

Delroy ‘Uzi’ Edwards, *Yardie hitman, described by a friend:*

‘If you mess with Delroy, he’ll kill you with a wink.’

Richard Loeb, *to police investigating the murder of fourteen year old Robert Franks, whom Loeb and his friend Nathan Leopold had killed:*

‘If I were going to pick out a boy to kidnap or murder, that’s just the kind of cocky little son-of-a-bitch I would pick.’

Richard Loeb's uncle, *when asked to settle the bill of lawyer Clarence Darrow, who had single-handedly saved Loeb and Nathan Leopold from the electric chair – after being begged to take on the case in the first place:*

‘You know Clarence, the world is full of eminent lawyers who would have paid a fortune for the chance to distinguish themselves in this case.’

Denis Nilsen, *the Muswell Hill serial killer, asked about the circumstances of one killing:*

‘End of the day, end of the drinking, end of a person.’

Fred West, *to detectives, about burying a victim in the back garden and finding the hole he had dug was too small:*

‘I thought “shit, I can't get her down there. I'm going to have to cut her up again”.’

Jim Dowsett, *speaking to the widow at the funeral of his business partner whom he had paid a hitman to murder:*

‘I wish I'd been able to shake his hand one last time. I shall never be able to go to the cemetery again.’

The Governor of Pentonville Prison, *on Timothy Evans, who was awaiting execution for the 10 Rillington Place murders, of which he was wrongly convicted:*

‘I don't think he is dull but he is the type often met with in the Army – fool enough to forge his leave-pass, short-sighted.’

Lucky Luciano:

‘The public is a bunch of crumbs askin' to be taken.’

Arnold Rothstein, *New York gambler and gangland boss of the 1920s, to a reporter:*

❛The majority of the human race are dubs and dumbells. They have rotten judgement and no brains and when you have learned to do things and how to size up people and dope out methods for yourself, they jump to the conclusion that you are crooked.❜

... Rothstein described by the night cashier at Lindy's, his favourite restaurant:

❛The way he talks you can stand beside him and not hear anything. Besides, who listens?❜

William Palmer, *Victorian serial killer, to the druggist who sold him his poison:*

❛If I poison a dog with strychnine, will there be any traces left in the stomach?❜

Charles Bravo, *later victim of an unsolved murder, when congratulated by a friend on his engagement to be married:*

❛Damn your congratulations.
I only want the money.❜

Charlie Starkweather, *sitting in the electric chair, asked if he would donate his eyes to the Lions Club eye bank:*

❛Hell no! No one ever did anything for me. Why in the hell should I do anything for anyone else?❜

Frank Vitkovic, *giving a clue as to the influences that led him to shoot eight people dead and wound five others in an Australian bank in 1987:*

❛I just like violent films. I don't know why. They make me feel better, all that violence gets me pumped up. The sound of the gun going "pow". It's the only fun I know.❜

...writing in his diary at the age of sixteen:

‘I know one thing for certain. I am hated very much by many people, but they don’t know anything of my hatred which is twice as much as theirs.’

Carl Panzram, *travelling robber and mass murderer:*

‘Whenever I met a hobo who wasn’t too rusty looking I would make him raise his hands and drop his pants. I wasn’t very particular either. I rode them old and young, tall and short, white and black.’

...in a letter from Death Row to lobbyists against capital punishment:

‘I wish you all had one neck – and I had my hands on it.’

Michel Henriot, *Frenchman who shot his wife five times with a hunting rifle as she tried to make a telephone call:*

‘I wanted the pleasure of shooting something new.’

George Smith, *‘Brides in the Bath’ killer, to the landlady in whose lodging house he had drowned his wife:*

‘When they are dead they are done with.’

Clay Allison, *killer-for-hire and drunkard who operated in New Mexico after the American War of Independence:*

‘I never killed man who didn’t need it.’

John Wayne Gacy, *on his 33 victims:*

‘Killing them was almost too easy. It was no challenge after the first dozen or so.’

Donald 'Tony the Greek' Frankos, *former freelance hitman:*

'The one thing I didn't love 100% was the killing, though I can't honestly say I hated it either. I killed because people I hung around respected hitters, and the reputation I acquired opened many doors for me. But I wasn't the type who got his thrills from murdering. I met plenty of these disgusting perverts, and sent a couple of them onto the next life.'

Joe Fischer, *World War II hero-cum hitman-cum serial killer, on his failure to adjust to normal living after the war:*

'Killing felt too good to stop.'

Henry Lee Lucas, *serial killer:*

'Killing someone is just like walking outdoors. If I wanted a victim, I'd just go get one. I didn't even consider a person a human being.'

Ronnie Kray, *recalling the murder that put him in prison for life:*

'I felt fucking marvellous. I have never felt so bloody alive, before or since. Twenty years on and I can recall every second of the killing of George Cornell.

I have replayed it in my mind millions of times.❜

Reggie Kray, *on his feelings after killing Jack 'The Hat' McVitie:*

❛I had a lot of nightmares. Not because I'd killed McVitie – one of the nastiest villains I have ever met – but because sticking a knife into anyone is not a pleasant thing to do. It would have been much easier and cleaner to have shot him.❜

Johann Hoch, *who married and murdered twenty four women in fifteen years, as he proposed to one of his sisters-in-law:*

❛Life is for the living. The dead are for the dead.❜

Joe Bonanno, *Mafia Godfather:*

❛To kill a rabbit, to kill a deer, to kill even a bear is simple. You aim steady and you shoot. But man is the hardest animal to kill. When you aim at a man, your hands shake, your eyes twitch, your heart flutters, your mind interferes. Man is the hardest animal to kill. If possible you should always touch the body with your gun to make sure the man is dead. If he gets away he will come back to kill you.❜

Charles Crimaldi, *hitman-cum-informer, on the reason why missing Teamsters Union leader Jimmy Hoffa's body would never be found:*

'Hoffa is now a goddamn hubcap. His body was crushed and smelted.'

Donald Hume, *who dropped the dismembered body of Stanley Setty from a plane into the sea – only for parts of it to be identified after it floated to the shore:*

'My victim's body followed me home.'

Lenny Maclean, *on his celebrated battle with rival, Roy Shaw:*

'I broke his jaw in seven places, bit half his ear off, half his cheekbone off, half his nose off and his bottom lip and then I'm going at him like a lunatic.'

Robert Stroud, *Birdman of Alcatraz, explaining the murder of a Leavenworth prison guard that kept him in solitary confinement from 1916 until his death in 1963:*

'The guard took sick and died all of a sudden. He died from heart trouble. I guess you would call it a puncture of the heart.'

Thomas Campbell, *Glasgow villain:*

'I've been stabbed, left for dead. I've been hit with axes, hatchets, steak knives, bone knives, swords, hammers...my whole body's covered in scars. So the thing is, if you're dealing with people who use these weapons then youneed to be prepared to fight on their rules. If they use a knife, you use a bigger knife. If they use a hammer, you use a hatchet. If you don't, you'll go under.'

Monk Eastman, *New York thug and crime boss:*

‘I likes to beat up a guy every now and then. It keeps me hand in.’

Bonnie Parker, *of Bonnie & Clyde, after shooting a policeman twice in the face:*

‘Look-a-there, his head bounced just like a rubber ball.’

Jack Henry Abbott:

‘For Americans to be shocked and disgusted at senseless murders and at crimes of extreme violence against the innocent is exactly identical to an old, worn-out prostitute expressing moral indignation at the thought of premarital sexual relations. Tell America that.’

Ted Bundy, *serial killer:*

‘I feel sorry for people who feel guilt. I feel sorry for people who are drug addicts or who are criminals. I feel sorry for business executives who have to lust after money and power. I feel sorry for a lot of people who have to do things that hurt them. But I don't feel sorry for anyone who doesn't feel guilt, because the guilt doesn't solve anything, really. It hurts you.’

David Copeland, *bomber of the Admiral Duncan pub in Soho, who killed three people and injured 139 others:*

‘My main intent was to spread fear, resenment and hatred throughout this country. I'd just be the spark, the spark that would set fire to this country, cos every nutter out there, if he wants to get on the news, he's gonna have to blow something up.’

Joseph Genite, *of the Black Hand Gang, in a demand to a wealthy Chicago businessman:*

‘You will be so good as to send me $2,000 if your life is dear to you. So I beg you warmly to put them (the small bills) on your door within four days. But, if not, I swear this week's time not even the dust of your family will exist. With regards, believe me to be your friend.’

Dr. Harold Shipman, *giving a death certificate to the relatives of one of his 215 victims:*

‘This is how we end up – just a piece of paper.’

...to police who questioned him about murdering his patients:

‘You don't understand medical matters. You are only plods.’

Ma, Pa and all the Family

Reggie Kray, *recalling his mother:*

‘She was the kindest woman in the world. She never hit us – not even when we’d been right little bastards. And whenever any of the neighbours or the mother of some kid we’d bashed up complained about us, she’d always say, “What, my twins? Never!” The thing was, she meant it. She thought the sun shone out of Ron and me.’

Ronnie Kray:

‘I would kill any man who spoke ill of my mother.’

Albert Donoghue, *Kray henchman:*

‘Wondering how much Ronnie and Reggie’s parents connived in their criminal activities, or if they knew what an evil, pair of brats they had reared, was like to solve the riddle of the Sphinx.’

Joe Fischer, *hit man and serial killer:*

‘If I could dig up my mother’s grave I’d take out her bones and kill her again.’

Wally Thompson, *old-time London villain:*

‘My father was a hansom-cab driver. Straight as a die. I was the only corkscrew in the family.’

Ronnie Knight, *speaking to The Sun newspaper in 1984, about his mother:*

‘My old mother, Nellie, is 83 and very ill with Parkinson’s disease.’

...and in 1994, also to The Sun:

‘She’s 87, has Parkinson’s disease and her mind is wandering.’

Ruby Sparks, *self-styled ‘Burglar to the Nobility’, on family pride:*

‘My Uncle Frank was a burglar and our family never saw any harm in that. But my mother did object to the way he smooched around in baggy trousers and his jersey a different colour under the arms, where sweat made it look as if a custard tart had melted there. “I expect him to toff himself up when he comes visiting here”, my mother said, “as we are very respected in this neighbourhood.”’

Salvatore Giuliano, *Sicilian bandit, in an appeal to the carabinieri who had imprisoned his mother:*

‘If you yourselves love your mammas and your country, refuse to fight in this fratricidal war. Do not be deceived by the proprietors of the press and your superiors, who call their war “a war against delinquency", because the war that they make against me should be called "a war against motherhood". Perhaps the reason for my success against this vast effort is due not only to my expertness but also to the Divine Hand whose aim is only one: To rein in those false prophets who want to destroy the greatest love that He defends for us, the most precious things of our lives, our mammas.❜

Angelo Bruno, *murdered Mafia Godfather, as recalled by his daughter:*

❛They never pinned anything on him. They couldn't prove he did anything wrong. He never dealt in drugs, he never dealt in prostitution, pornography or murder. Even his speech was clean.❜

Violet Kray, *mother of the infamous twins:*

❛If you've got to choose between your boys and the police, what choice is that, especially if they're all you've got?❜

...on the twins:

❛Both of them was good boys at heart. I knew the things people said about them couldn't be true, anyhow.❜

Victoria Gotti, *daughter of John, the Teflon Don:*

❛My father is the last of the Mohicans.❜

Jimmy O'Connor, *on his childhood in London of the 1920s:*

❛I thought my parents were proud of me being a good little tea-leaf, but my mother wasn't. She thought I ought to join the Boy Cubs.❜

Hugh Collins, *on ending up doing life for murder:*

‘I don’t think my family could have changed anything. Perhaps if one of them had had enough insight to see what was lying ahead, and had told me the truth about things.’

Chopper Read, *Australian criminal turned celebrity, on fatherhood:*

‘People come along and they say Chopper this and Chopper that, Chopper everything else. But I’m just Charlie’s dad and I don’t feel very Chopperish.’

Jimmy Boyle, *on his upbringing in the Glasgow Gorbals:*

‘It was usual in our street to have your big brother to protect you, but my eldest brother was a fashion designer, a homosexual, and the next one had an accident when an iron railing fell and broke his skull, so neither of them could fight. I had to do the battles for all us boys. My Ma got a job cleaning out the trams when my father died. She was always worried about us getting into trouble. She was a Catholic. We all were. I used to go to confession and tell about my thieving to the priest and I felt a lot better for it.’

Charles Kray:

‘All through our lives I’ve tried to do the best for my brothers, but unfortunately they don’t see it that way. I’m their human punchbag, the scapegoat who gets the blame every time something goes wrong. They even give me the impression that it is my fault they’re in prison...Elder brother

Charlie was, alas, always a bit too soft for their liking. They might not care to admit it, but when it comes down to it they view me as a great disappointment.❜

...on his twin brothers:

❛I've heard stories about what they were that make me want to throw up. About them being terrible. They wasn't. They were little gentlemen and everybody said so.❜

❛...Some of the rubbish that's been said and written about me and my brothers over the years has given me the right hump.❜

Graham Young, *the St Albans Poisoner, on using his family as guinea pigs:*

❛I chose my family because they were close at hand, where I could observe and note the results of my experiments. I love my antimony, I love the power it gives me.❜

Ellen Dunne *of Dublin, interviewed on television in 1984 about allegations that her sons were the drug godfathers of Ireland:*

❛My sons are all gentlemen – beautiful men, beautiful manners, beautiful bodies.❜

Joseph Bonnano, *Mafia boss, to his son, Bill:*

‘Don’t be the first to dirty our name. Our name has been clean so long, for so many generations.’

Al Capone, *speaking from Alcatraz:*

‘My boy thinks I’m in Europe. Whenever he sees a picture of a big boat he asks his mother if it’s bringing daddy home.’

Altagracia Ramirez Navas, *father of Carlos the Jackal, following his son’s capture in 1994:*

‘My son is the greatest there is in the world.... My boy is radical but he is also sweet.’

Maria Giuliano, *mother of the Sicilian bandit known as ‘Turridu’, expressing surprise that her son had been shot dead while sleeping by an informer, Gaspare Pisciotta:*

‘Pisciotta and Giuliano were blood brothers and wrote their names with drops of each other’s blood. Pisciotta became a traitor, worse than Cain. His heart was always bad and Turridu’s was open and generous. My son Turridu often had to tie Pisciotta to a tree and beat him, to teach him manners.’

William Bentley, *on the scenes outside Wandsworth Prison following the execution of his son Derek for a murder he did not commit:*

‘To such public indignation, the baby I had helped to deliver just over nineteen years before went out of this world.’

Rusty Rastelli, *boss of the Bonanno crime family, speaking of his wife who was murdered after informing on him to the FBI:*

‘Hey – you play, you gotta pay,’

The Marquis de Bernardy, *French criminal, on being told that the body of his wife, whom he was later convicted of murdering, had been found:*

‘One always wishes to know where the dead are resting.’

Joyce Dernley, *widow of Syd, Britain's last hangman:*

‘My husband was a very unassuming man, fond of a joke and a pint of beer. He was very popular.’

Mrs Ethel Christie, *on hearing her husband, the 10 Rillington Place killer, John Christie – who would later also kill her – called a murderer:*

‘Don't you dare call my husband a murderer, he's a good man.’

George Smith, *the 'Brides in the Bath' murderer, in a post card to his father-in-law:*

‘Sir – in answer to your application concerning my parentage, etc. My mother was a bus-horse, my father a cab-driver, my sister a rough-rider over the Arctic regions – my brothers were all gallant sailors on a steam-roller.’

Alfred de Marigny, *acquitted of the murder of Sir Harry Oakes, asked who had killed him, by a reporter:*

‘I do not know. I was tried ten per cent for killing Sir Harry and ninety per cent for marrying Sir Harry's daughter.’

Butch Witte, *aged fifteen, asked by police how he felt about killing his grandmother with a crossbow:*

‘I felt neutral about it. I didn't care one way or the other.’

Albert Caesar Tocco, *Chicago gangster described by an informant in the 1980s:*

‘Usually you don’t hurt the families. But he would throw it out a window if it was up to him – the wife, the family, their cats and dogs. Whatever it took. He was very vicious.’

George Lamson, *poisoner, passing a lethal capsule to his brother-in-law:*

‘Percy, you are a champion pill-taker, take this.’

Abe ‘Kid Twist’ Reles’ mother-in-law, *asked if she knew that the Murder Inc. hitman was a killer:*

‘A killer? No – he was very good around the house.’

Ed Kemper, *asked why he had killed his grandmother:*

‘I just wondered how it would feel to shoot grandma.’

Peter Hogg, *told by police that his wife’s remains had been discovered in a lake by an amateur diver:*

‘That was unlucky, wasn’t it?’

Killer Women, Wives and Molls

Arsenic Annie Doss, *asked why she had murdered four of her five husbands:*

‘I was searching for the perfect mate, the real romance of life.’

Penny Bjorkland, *hitch hiker who fired eighteen bullets into an innocent driver who gave her a lift, on being sentenced to life imprisonment in California:*

‘This is not what I expected. I consider myself a normal, average girl.’

Helene Jagado, *French maid who poisoned seventeen victims during her work in French households:*

‘Wherever I go, people die.’

Virginia Hill, *New York gangster's moll, asked by a senator what made her a favourite of the underworld:*

‘Senator, I'm the best goddamned cocksucker in the world.’

...to reporters following the murder of her lover, Bugsy Siegel:

‘His name wasn't Bugsy Siegel. It was Ben. Ben Siegel. And he was no gangster – what do you know? Why, that man loved poetry. There was a poem both of us kept... Aw you jerks wouldn't understand it anyway!’

Charlotte Bryant, *in a telegram to King George V from the death cell at Exeter Prison:*

‘Mighty King, have pity on your lowly, afflicted subject. Don't let them kill me on Wednesday... From the brink of the cold, dark grave, I, a poor, helpless woman ask you not to let them kill me. I am innocent.’

Margaret Allen, *lesbian bus-conductress, awaiting execution for murder in 1949:*

‘I shall be dead on Wednesday. It would help if I could cry but my manhood holds back my tears.’

Ruth Ellis, *to her solicitor, shortly before she was due to be hanged for the murder of her lover, David Blakely:*

‘I gave David a lot of rope – come to think about it, he's giving me quite a bit now.’

Louisa Merrifield, *Blackpool murderess, three days before her victim died, speaking to a friend:*

‘We're landed! I went to live with an old lady and she died and left me the bungalow worth £4,000.’

Edith Chubb, *who killed her overbearing sister-in-law:*

‘I felt irritated by the way she put her tea-cup down.’

Noeleen Hendley, *who hired a man named Paul Buxton to murder her husband, when asked why she had appeared on television, pleading for help in finding her husband's killer:*

‘I forgot it was Paul Buxton.’

Rosemary West, *to police, on being told her husband Fred had implicated her in the murder of their eldest daughter:*

‘Put it this way, he’s a dead man if I ever get my hands on him.’

...told by police that the garden and patio at 25 Cromwell Street was to be dug up:

‘There’s nothing you will stop at is there?’

Lea Papin, *French servant (she and her sister Christine were dubbed “Les Diaboliques, the Devils of Le Mans”) on murdering their employers:*

‘I would rather have had my mistresses’ skins than they had ours.’

Ellen Cannon, *wife of London villain, Joe Cannon:*

‘From what I’ve heard and read, the public idea of a villain’s wife is a brassy blonde with rings all over her fingers, dressed up to the nines in very bad taste, enjoying the good life when her man is doing the business and living in the lap of luxury when he is paying the penalty for his crimes in one or other of Her Majesty’s prisons. This is a load of old rubbish.’

Marilyn Wisbey, *self-styled gangster’s moll:*

‘It’s the women who are the real heroes in gangland. They are the ones who have to stay behind and go out when they’re taken out.’

Kathryn Kelly, *wife of “Machine Gun” Kelly, after being sentenced to life in Oklahoma City:*

‘My pekinese dog would have gotten a life sentence in this court.’

Marthe Watts, *associate of the Messina brothers, London vice barons of the 40s and 50s:*

"In the course of plying my trade on the streets of London I have had more than 400 convictions as what you call a "common prostitute". Why "common" I do not know. You do not, after all, call your burglars "common burglars"."

Starr Faithfull, *whose death at sea in 1931 remains unsolved:*

"If one wants to get away with murder one has to jolly well keep one's wits about one. It's the same with suicide."

Sue Butterworth, *ex-stripper, serving life for killing a neighbour in a row over a video recorder:*

"I used to work on the doors in the seedy clubs, drawing in the punters. I was good at it too. I'd always wear some scanty-looking number with black stockings and suspenders. I'd stand outside the club calling 'Rub your tummy, guv'nor! Step inside – live show!"

Cynthia Payne, *brothel keeper:*

"I'd say lots of women actually admire me for running a brothel. I found out a local meeting that some of the street girls are even doing it in people's front gardens these days."

Mary Goode, *New York brothel-keeper, asked in court to define what she described as a "respectable disorderly house":*

"Well, a respectable house can be run, for instance, by a woman who only lets gentlemen in. She never lets gunmen in or convicts."

Ellen Kelly, *to her bushranger son, Ned, as he was about be hanged in Melbourne:*

‘Mind you die like a Kelly, Ned.’

Edith Thompson, *murderess, describing, in a letter to her lover, how she had put a broken electric-light bulb in her husband's porridge:*

‘I used a lot. Big pieces too.’

Joyce Turner, *mother of six, on murdering her ‘lazy good for nothing bum’ husband:*

‘He always wanted to die in bed. I merely arranged it, that's all.’

Bonnie Parker, *asked by an irate Clyde Barrow why she had not shot a man who had almost prevented their getaway by throwing a log under the car:*

‘Why honey, I wasn't going to kill that nice old man. He was white headed.’

...as she showed her mother a photograph of herself and Clyde Barrow:

‘When they shoot us, don't ever say anything ugly about Clyde.’

Chicago May Sharpe, *well-known in America, London and Paris in the early years of the century, who exploited her beauty to blackmail men:*

‘I caught them all – university professors, ministers, priests, gamblers, country yokels, sports, gentle folk and visiting grandees from foreign parts.’

‘...My old friends in the police write me letters of encouragement. Christians feel called upon to send me platitudes. Reformers insist upon drawing their pet theories to my attention. Professional crooks berate and praise me. Beggars importune me. Sycophants lather me with adulation. The rich – and others – patronise me.’

Manette, *French murderess, who went to the guillotine in 1808, to the executioner:*

‘Don’t you think it’s a pity to cut off a head as beautiful as mine.’

Aileen Wuornos, *the first American convicted serial killer:*

‘I’m not a man-hating lesbian who only killed to rob, robbed to kill. This is a downright fabrication, full of fairy tales and very far from the truth, all for a fast buck. A sick and vile made-up horror flick these law-enforcement officers have created. They’ve already set it up for a real profound box office hit.’

Susan Atkins, *on Charles Manson:*

‘He is the king and I am his queen. The queen does what the king says. The king? look at his name, Manson. “Man’s son.” Now I have visible proof of God, proof the Church never gave me.’

Irene Schroeder, *asked if she had any last wish as she was strapped into the electric chair, days before her lover Glen Dagus, for the murder of a policeman:*

‘Yes, there is something. Tell them in the kitchen to fry Glen’s eggs on both sides. He likes them that way.’

Kate Howard, *on her former husband, Ronnie Kray:*

‘Ron has a way with women, he’s a right old charmer when he wants to be. The smiling viper I call him.’

. . .on informing her father of her plans to marriage plans :

‘“By the way Dad, I’m marrying Ronnie Kray.” He stopped mowing then he looked at me as if to say: “Oh my God, what’s she doing now?” Then he went on mowing.’

Mary Kinder, *mistress of John Dillinger:*

‘Johnny’s just an ordinary fellow. Of course he goes out and holds up banks and things, but he’s really just like any other fellow.’

Glenys Brown, wife of Wembley Mob bank robber **Bruce Brown**, *to police who asked why her husband’s wardrobe included two balaclava helmets:*

‘For skiing, of course.’

Pearl O’ Loughlin, *convicted of murdering her step-daughter:*

‘You can’t hang me if I don’t confess. You don’t think I’ve been a detective’s wife for two years for nothing.’

Trouble with Women...

Al Capone:

‘The trouble with women today is their excitement over too many things outside the home. A woman’s home and her children are her real happiness. If she would stay there, the world would have less to worry about the modern woman.’

Sam Giancana, *Mafia Godfather:*

‘Women are like shoes. Wear them out, throw them away. It’s nice if they’re the best lookin’ shoes you can buy, but they’re still shoes any way you cut it...disposable.’

Pete Gillett, *friend of the Krays:*

‘Women get a kick out of being involved with a criminal. You get women that like to be around villainous type guys. They enjoy the adrenaline and being seen with the faces. I don’t want to seem a braggart but I’m talking about personal experience. When I came out of jail, I was in the papers and on television. I got besieged by them, one came up and grabbed me by the bollocks and said, “You won’t have had sex for years” – wallop. I freaked right out.’

Henri Landru's *prosecutor, at the defence suggestion that his client had not murdered women, but had shipped them off to brothels:*

‘What? Women who were all over fifty years of age? Women whose false hair, false teeth, false bosoms, as well as identity papers, you, Landru, have kept and we captured?’

Edwin Bartlett, *whose wife Adelaide was to murder him by poison:*

‘One ought to have two wives, one to take out and one to do the work.’

J. Edgar Hoover *on Ma Barker, matriarch of the infamous Barker Gang:*

‘She kept open house for big-time criminality. With the calm of a person ordering a meal she brought about bank robberies, hold-ups or kidnappings and commanded the slaying of persons who, only a short time before, had enjoyed what they thought was her friendship. Yet withal, she shuddered in jealous trepidation when a new gun moll threatened to steal the love of one of her boys, and she was one of the easiest weepers in the history of criminality. She liked now and then to hum hymns... She gave nearly half her lifetime to a defiance of the law and died still hating it, a bullet-heated machine gun in her aged hands.’

...in 1938:

‘Several years ago thousands of our citizens shivered in fear of a kidnapper whose name had much to do with the terror he engendered: he was called “Machine Gun” Kelly. However, there was someone far more dangerous than “Machine Gun”

Kelly. That was "Machine Gun" Kelly's wife...If ever there was hen-pecked man it was George "Machine Gun" Kelly.❞

Marc Lepine, *arriving at Montreal University to begin a massacre that left fourteen women students dead and many more seriously wounded:*

❝I am here to fight against feminism.❞

...in a letter written before he embarked on his anti-feminism massacre:

❝Feminists always have a talent to enrage me. They want to keep the advantages of women (e.g., cheaper insurance, extended maternity leave...) while trying to grab those of the men. Thus, it is an obvious truth that if the Olympic Games removed the Men-Women distinction, there would be women only in the graceful events. So the feminists are not fighting to remove that barrier. They are so opportunistic they neglect to profit from the knowledge accumulated by men through the ages. They always try to misrepresent them every time they can. Thus the other day I heard they were honouring the Canadian men and women who fought at the front line during the world wars How can you explain then that women were not authorised to go to the front line.❞

Willie Sutton, *bank robber:*

❝Thieves have always had an affinity for prostitutes. They're around, they're available, and they're disposable. And maybe underneath all the rationalisation most thieves believe it's as good as they deserve.❞

Donald 'Pee Wee' Gaskins, *serial killer, while on Death Row awaiting execution:*

'I never heard of no women-libbers demanding their equal rights when it comes to capital punishment.'

Maurice O' Mahoney, *London robber of the 1970s, whose wife locked him out if he wasn't home at night:*

'I often used to return in the early hours after a successful evening of villainy and find the door locked and bolted like Fort Knox. She had so many security devices on the inside of the front door that there was no way I could get in once she had locked it. I would bang, shout and ring the bell, I often woke the whole street, but she just lay in bed, determined to make me suffer.'

John Gosling, *head of Scotland Yard's Vice Squad in the 1950s, on prostitutes:*

'Their faces go before their time, their skin coarsens, their speech turns foul until at last it is true to say that they are almost completely de-womanised in every gentle aspect of that word. This, like the mark of Cain on the brow of the murderer, is the stigmata of prostitution which none can escape.'

Giovanni Falcone, *anti-Mafia investigator:*

'There is nothing more dishonourable for a Sicilian than prostitution, and even more for a man of honour. That's why, in complete contrast to what happens on the other side of the Atlantic, this activity does not appear in the balance sheets of our Mafia.'

Sam Miller, *US lawyer, blaming client Judd Gray's predicament on the influence of his lover, Ruth Snyder, who stood co-accused of her husband's murder:*

‘The tale of my client is the most tragic story that ever gripped the human heart. He was dominated by a cold, heartless, calculating mastermind and master will. He was a helpless mendicant of a designing, deadly, conscienceless, abnormal woman, a human serpent, a human fiend in the guise of a woman. He became inveigled and drawn into this hopeless chasm when reason was gone, when manhood was gone, and when his mind was weakened by lust and passion.’

William F. Howe, *New York lawyer, addressing to the jury in the case of a girl accused of murdering her lover:*

‘Look, gentlemen! Look into this poor creatures face! Does she look like a guilty woman? No, a thousand times no! Those are the tears of innocence and shame! Send her back to her aged father to comfort his old age. Let him clasp her and press his trembling lips to her hollow eyes! Let him wipe away her tears and bid her sin no more!’

Monk Eastman, *New York gangster, to police who arrested him for beating up a girl he had taken to a restaurant:*

‘It ain't nothin' officer. Rosie here ain't as dainty as she could be. She made a pig of herself. I told her not to wipe her nose wit da tablecloth. Manners is important! Anyway, I only gave her a little poke, just enough to put a shanty on her glimmer. But I always takes off me knucks first.’

Clyde Barrow, *on his partner, Bonnie Parker's coolness under fire:*

'That Bonnie, she's sure full of piss and vinegar.'

Phil Kaufman, *former jail mate of Charles Manson:*

'Susan Atkins was the pretty one, just too feminine, so to take her down a peg he named her Sadie Glutz. Now she says she's sorry, she's found Jesus. Shit, they've all found Jesus – that's the best way to get out of jail.'

Harry Pitts, *speaking after the death of his mother, Shirley, known in the London underworld as the Queen of the Shoplifters:*

'She was more of a man than most men.'

Ronnie Knight, *on his second wife, Barbara Windsor:*

'I fancied her so much my front teeth ached. There she stood, all beaming smiles and coy glances...Any man who denied lusting after those voluptuous boobs was either a liar or bent as a spaniel's hind leg.'

*...***Knight***'s third wife, Sue, on the same Ms Windsor:*

'She is a three foot peroxide blonde dwarf. At least I've got all my own hair.'

Charles Ellsom, *at his Old Bailey trial for the murder of his girlfriend:*

'A fortune teller told me the gallows were in my cards and that she was the girl I would swing for.'

Dr. Harold Shipman, *attempting to explain the murder of a patient:*

'I turned round to get my stethoscope out of my bag and she just collapsed and died.'

Friends...and Enemies

Bill Fullerton, *leader of the Billy Boys, a Glasgow gang of the 1920s, recalling a gang member's wedding:*

‘The bridegroom stood before the minister with a sword concealed in his morning dress. The best man had a gun in his pocket. I'll never forget the scene as they left the church. The gang waiting outside threw bottles instead of confetti.’

Frank Costello, *known as "Prime Minister of the Underworld", declining FBI chief J. Edgar Hoover's invitation to join him for a cup of coffee:*

‘I got to be careful of my associates. They'll be accusing me of consorting with questionable characters.’

...to a name dropper who claimed to know Frank Sinatra:

‘I know you know Sinatra, but does Sinatra know you?’

...after being shot at point blank range:

‘I didn't see nothin'. I was facing the other way when I was shot. I haven't an enemy in the world.’

Judith Exner, *lover of Frank Sinatra and John F. Kennedy, as well as Mafia Godfather, Sam Giancana:*

‘I didn't know then that Sam was the Chicago Godfather. But I did know he was important to Frank because of the way Sinatra acted around him, bowing and scraping and being so deferential.❞

Jimmy 'The Weasel' Fratianno, *on Frank Sinatra's associations with Mafia figures:*

❝He likes "made" guys. He likes to be around them. He likes to have pictures taken with them. Look at all the publicity: Giancana, Lucky Luciano, the Fiscettis, Gambino, myself! He thrives on the stuff, I'm telling you. Of course, he ain't gonna tell that to the president.❞

Ronnie Biggs, *Great Train Robber, recalling his rescue from Wandsworth Prison by Paul Seabourne:*

❝I saw the top of Paul's stockinged head appear and almost immediately the first of the two rope ladders came snaking over the wall. We ran forward as the second one came down, then, suddenly, I froze, somehow unable to start climbing. I don't know why, I just froze on the spot for a split second until someone shouted "Get going Biggsie," and I started climbing fast. Paul was at the top of the wall sitting there with an axe in his hand ready to chop the ladders loose. He greeted me with "Hello, you big ugly bastard!"❞

Blackie Audett, *on his former partner,Charles "Pretty Boy" Floyd:*

"He was quite a kid. Good-looking, easy-going and a playboy. He like the girls a lot. And the girls liked him. He spent his money like a drunken Indian when he had it."

Motto *of Ragen's Colts, Chicago gang of the early 1900s:*

"Hit me and you hit 2,000."

Albert Anastasia, *recommending the murder of associate, Willie Moretti, whose eccentric behaviour and fondness of talking was causing underworld concern:*

"It should be a mercy killing."

Jimmy Boyle, *on his one-time friendship with the Krays:*

"I have always noticed an innate disdain by lots of Scottish guys for the English criminals – most of them thought they were a bit soft. This is certainly far from the truth, as the majority lived very tough lives but concentrated on cash, whereas we in Scotland were more inclined to weigh things up from the physical side."

Lord Boothby, *refuting allegations of a relationship with Ronnie Kray:*

"I am not a homosexual. I have not been to a Mayfair party of any kind for more than twenty years. I have met the man who is alleged to be a "king of the underworld" only three times, on business matters, and then by appointment in my flat, at his request, and in the company of other people. In short the whole affair is a tissue of atrocious lies."

Ronnie Kray, *on Lord Boothby:*

‘Silly old queen.’

Albert Donaghue, *Kray gang member, on Ronnie's homosexual relationship with Boothby:*

‘Boys will be boys, especially Tory politicians with a taste for rough trade.’

Leslie Payne, *on his former business associate Ronnie Kray:*

‘He was mad about celebrities, perhaps because their company proved his importance. Often, too, the point of the occasion would be a group photo, which he would use later in some scheme or other. But when, say, on the few occasions he was with Lord Boothby or Sonny Liston, he would just sit with his mouth open, staring. This was not intended to be rude: he just had no small talk beyond – “What are you going to ‘ave to drink?” or “Well, do you want a fag, then?”’

Mad Frankie Fraser, *on his former associates, the Krays:*

‘The Twins could be a bit difficult. One day they could be plotting to kill that glass on the table because it didn't shine. Next day it'd be something else.’

..on South London gangleader, Charlie Richardson:

‘The trouble with Charlie was, he was a kind man. He hadn't done proper bird and so he never really appreciated how the low life thought.’

Chopper Read, *on the transition from Australian hoodlum to best-selling author and hit movie:*

❛It's very socially isolating, you know. People, they like to talk to me. They like to say hello, they like to get the autograph, they like to get a photo taken. But they don't want me sitting in their lounge.❜

Freddie Foreman, *on the allegation that he was paid by the Krays to kill Frank 'The Mad Axeman' Mitchell:*

❛I had no need to kill anybody for money. I was doing alright. I did it as a favour for the twins. He was a nuisance.❜

Lucky Luciano, *on his friendship with Frank Costello, Meyer Lansky and Bugsy Siegel:*

❛We was the best team that ever got put together. We knew our jobs better than any other guys in the street. We was like the Four Horsemen of Notre Dame – except what would two Jewish guys be doin' at Notre Dame?❜

John Steele, *Glasgow villain, on receiving advice as a youth from one of his father's gangster friends, Toe Elliott:*

❛"Listen to me as a friend and don't waste your life in gaols," Toe said. He couldn't sit still, and as he moved about I could see that he had a gun in the waistband of his suit trousers. He was dressed like a tailor's dummy with his fancy suit. He was very small, yet even so he had all my attention. He was a character, and I had to respect him for trying to make me see sense. He said that the police had been after my dad for years, and if they couldn't get him then they would get me, to hit back at my dad. I had heard this many times but it didn't mean anything to me, since I didn't know what my dad had done in the past that was so bad. Before Toe left he gave me twenty pounds for a night out at the dancing: I bought a tool kit for break-ins with the money.’

Ian Brady, *Moors Murderer, on his relationship with Myra Hindley:*

‘A meshing into one took place. We didn't need to speak. Just a gesture – something had got to be done, something would happen...It was so close, we knew exactly what was in each other's mind. We were one mind.’

Dr Crippen, *as described by his friend the actor, Seymour Hicks:*

‘In looking at him I was by no means sure I was not talking to a bream or a mullet.’

Wilfred Macartney, *on his fellow prisoner, the robber, Ruby Sparks:*

‘Ruby was one of the most reliable men it has been my fortune to meet – shrewd, able and energetic. He is of a type that our present society seems unable to use to the advantage of society as a whole. It turns people like Ruby Sparks into motor bandits and makes paranoiacs like Hitler and Goering the arbiters of the destinies of millions.’

Marc Lepine, *Canadian anti-feminist mass killer, described by his flat-mate:*

‘Doing favours was his way of expressing his affection.’

Jamie Petrolini, *teenage random killer who put all the blame on his friend and co-accused:*

‘Richard Elsey was the murderer and I was just the knife... He is the reason I am Public Enemy Number Two.’

Carlos Lehder, *on hospitality:*

‘On my island in the Bahamas I told my people when any Latin lands, give him whatever he needs, no matter what he is running.’

Ned Kelly, *Australian bushranger, asked why he had walked into a police trap to try to rescue his friends:*

‘A man would be a nice sort of a dingo to walk out on his mates.’

Two-Gun Louis Alterie, *to reporters at the funeral of gangster/florist, Dion O'Banion:*

‘I have no idea who killed Deanie, but I would die smiling if only I had chance to meet the guys who did, at any time and any place they mention and I would get at least two or three of them before they got me. If I knew who killed Deanie I'd shoot it out with the gang of killers before the sun rose in the morning and some of us, maybe all of us, would be lying on slabs in the undertaker's place.’

A police sergeant, *commenting on the location of gangster Tony Genna's grave in a Chicago cemetery, only feet away from that of his enemy Dion O'Bannion:*

‘When Judgement Day comes and those graves are open there'll be hell to pay in this cemetery.’

Jimmy Hoffa, *mobster leader of the Teamsters Union, on Attorney General Robert Kennedy:*

‘Robert F. Kennedy was a man who always made a big thing out of how strong and how tough he was, how he had been a football player or something at Harvard and how he always exercised and kept himself in top shape... I was sure that Kennedy was a hard-nosed guy who was so spoiled all his life that he had to have his way in everything no matter who got hurt. The kind of guy you had to be as nasty with as he was with you or he'd run right over you. But it's always been my theory that you keep the door open to your enemies. You know all about your friends.’

...to a fellow Teamsters Union official on his hatred for the President's brother:

‘Somebody needs to bump that son of a bitch off. Bobby Kennedy has got to go.’

Sam Giancana, *Chicago Godfather, irritated by the constant surveillance by government agents, and alluding to Frank Sinatra:*

‘If Bobby Kennedy wants to talk to me I'll be glad to talk to him and he knows who to go through.’

Clyde Barrow:

‘Machine Gun Kelly? I've forgotten more about a tommy gun than that phony creep ever knew!’

Bugs Moran, *on his rival bootlegger* **Al Capone**:

‘The Beast uses his musclemen to peddle rot-gut alcohol and green beer. I'm a legitimate salesman of good beer and pure whisky. He trusts nobody and suspects everybody. He always has guards. I travel around with a couple of pals. The Behemoth can't sleep nights. If you ask me, he's on dope. Me, I don't even need an aspirin.’

Spike O'Donnell, *Chicago bootlegger:*

‘I can whip this bird Capone anytime he wants to step out in the open and fight like a man.’

Dutch Schultz, *on his rival Legs Diamond:*

‘I don't trust Legs. He gets excited and starts pulling a trigger like another guy wipes his nose.’

Legs Diamond, *on Schultz:*

‘I don't trust the Dutchman. He's a crocodile. He's sneaky.’

An **FBI agent** *on Danny Greene, who claimed Irish descent and was murdered by the Cleveland Mafia:*

‘He had a green Lincoln, he wrote in green ink, he had a green flag in front of his house. Everything about him was green. He would get on television and call the La Cosa Nostra figures maggots. He felt he was indestructible.’

Big Bill Dwyer, *bootlegger, on the up-and-coming Legs Diamond.*

‘He's nothing but a river pirate come to New York City. That no-good son-of-a-bitch will get his if it's the last thing I do.’

Valerio Viccei, *Knighsbridge robber, on his displeasure at film director Michael Winner's portrayal of him in a television drama:*

‘He made me out to be a complete idiot, but I will always remember him and call him Underpants Michael.’

Ian Brady, *Moors Murderer, referring to* **Sunday Express** *columnist, Brian Hitchen, who he claimed had injured his feelings:*

‘I shall hunt the quarry to perdition and beyond with the same commitment as Captain Ayab did Moby Dick.’

Vito Genovese, *Mafia boss, to soon-to-be informer, Joe Valachi – before giving him the kiss of death:*

‘You know, sometimes if I had a barrel of apples, and one of these apples is touched...not all rotten but just a little touched...it has to be removed or it will touch all the rest of the apples.’

Charles Bronson, *said to be Britain's most disruptive prisoner, on leaving Broadmoor:*

‘You should have seen the send-off when I finally walked out of there! As I was led out of Norfolk House, the loonies were at the windows, shouting and waving little Union Jacks. I couldn't believe it. The flags were obviously given to them by the staff.’

Doc Moran, *shortly before he was murdered by fellow members of the Barker-Karpis Gang:*

‘I've got this gang in the hollow of my hand.’

Carmine Galante, *New York mafioso, described by a former associate:*

‘If he was walking with one person, you'd learn not to join him as a third. He'd pick a fight with the third person and force the second to become his ally.’

Bob King, *London armed robber, on prison officers:*

‘When I was sixteen or seventeen I just hated screws. I would gladly have mown them down with machine guns, cut their toes off with hacksaw blades. I hated them mortally.’

Captured!

Sid Vicious, *of the Sex Pistols, to New York police officers apprehending him for the murder of his girlfriend Nancy Spungeon:*

‘You can’t arrest me. I’m a rock ’n’ roll star.’

Valerio Viccei, *the Knightsbridge £60 million robber, to Scotland Yard Flying Squad detectives:*

‘It’s only a game. You have won.’

George Lemay, *Canadian arch-criminal, arrested in 1965 after his photograph appeared in an early satellite TV programme:*

‘How did you people catch me? I seldom make mistakes.’

Tommaso Buscetta, *‘Godfather of Two Worlds’, to Brazilian police in Sao Paulo:*

‘If you’ve come to discuss my freedom, I’ll start with a million dollars. If you’ve come to question me I’ll say nothing.’

Major William Lemus, *of the Medellin police:*

‘The Virgin has smiled on us. We have captured Carlos Lehder.’

Duane ‘Dog’ Chapman, *US bounty hunter, to a fugitive captured at gunpoint:*

‘Six men can carry you or twelve men can judge you.’

Carlos Lehder, *Columbian drug baron, offered a cigarette by a DEA agent after his arrest:*

‘No thank you, I only smoke marijuana.’

Rafael Leon Rodriguez, *Miami drug importer, apologising for shooting at the detective who arrested him:*

‘Your job was to catch me.
My job was to get away.’

Sammy Lewis, *jailed drug dealer, on being apprehended by the Metropolitan Police:*

‘One minute it was nice and peaceful, the next I was surrounded by cops. They had my trousers down – but I was clean as a whistle. Didn’t even have a fart to give them.’

Howard Marks, *drug smuggler, on media interest in him after he was jailed for 25 years in America:*

‘The fame I’d longed for ever since I was a weak swot in school was now well and truly mine. I loved it.’

Dion O’Bannion, *Chicago gangster, to reporters after he and Hymie Weiss had been acquitted of burglary by a bribed jury, despite leaving fingerprints:*

‘It was an oversight. Hymie was supposed to wipe off the prints and he forgot.’

Leon Murant, *recaptured while reading a newspaper report of his escape from a French prison:*

‘I never had time to get to the end of the article.’

Maria Vincent, *cabaret artist and husband of French gangster Sami Khoury, to reporters after their joint arrest on drug charges:*

‘This is the most formidable publicity I've ever had – and no agent to pay.’

Marilyn Wisbey, *self-styled gangster's moll:*

‘When you come home from the abortion clinic, you don't need a visit from the Drugs Squad.’

Bruce Brown, *leader of London's Wembley Mob in the early 1970s, arrested for a series of bank robberies:*

‘My reputation has gone, my good name at the golf club, everything...’

Judd Gray, *charged in New York with the murder of his lover's husband:*

‘My word, gentlemen. When you know me better you'll see how ridiculous it is for a man like me to be in the clutches of the law. Why, I've never even been given a ticket for speeding.’

Henri Landru, *French serial killer:*

‘Oh! Fancy accusing me of being an assassin. That's too much. For it could mean a man's head!’

John Haigh, *who dissolved six victims in a drum of sulphuric acid:*

‘How can you prove murder if there is no body?’

John Faletico, *New York policeman, on the arrest of David Berkowitz, 'Son of Sam':*

'He had that stupid smile on his face, like it was a kid's game.'

Frederick Browne *who, along with William Kennedy, murdered PC Gutteridge in Essex in 1927, to police who arrested him:*

'What I can see of it, I shall have to get a machine gun for you bastards next time.'

Luciano Leggio, *head of the Corleone Mafia, to Sicilian police who arrested him at the age of thirty eight:*

'What could you want with me? I'm getting old. If you intend to keep me alive, you'll have to take me to a place in the sun.'

Nonce Lucarotti, *French gangster, to police who arrested him in 1959:*

'By arresting me you are depriving France of the honest citizen I wanted to become.'

George Russell, *betraying himself to the police officer who arrested him:*

'Did I murder this poor woman for something she was supposed to have and had not?'

Charles Makley, *of the Dillinger Gang, to police after his arrest:*

'Look at my dad, he worked like the devil all his life and what did he get out of it? I've lived as long in forty minutes at times as my dad did in forty years.'

Frank 'Jelly' Nash, *of the Dillinger Gang, offering his toupee to an FBI agent who arrested him:*

'I paid $100 for it in Chicago.'

Texas Ranger's warning after
Bonnie and Clyde *had been hit with 167 bullets:*

"Be careful, they may not be dead."

Vincent Ciucci, *arrested after chloroforming his wife and three children, shooting them all in the head and setting fire to their home:*

"How could a man kill his own children?"

Howard Unruh, *to police who arrested him for shooting dead thirteen people in twelve minutes:*

"I'm no psycho. I have a good mind."

Harry Roberts, *police killer, recalling his time on the run:*

"I was always having problems with my guns. Whenever I was out they were forever dropping on the ground or slipping through my waist band and down my trouser leg."

Ronnie Kray, *on the witnesses who gave evidence against him and his brothers:*

"At the end of the day, if you really analyse it, we were done for by an ex-boxer with a dodgy ticker and a brainless barmaid who fell for a copper's charm. After that it was going to be downhill all the way."

Jim Marshall, *Scotland Yard detective, to whom supergrass Bertie Smalls offered information on major crimes:*

‘When Bertie said he might be able to help us I knew he was wriggling. He knew he was caught bang to rights. I remember saying to myself as I watched his lips move: “No. You’re the best robber I’ll ever capture – fuck yer.”’

Jack Slipper, *Scotland Yard detective, who became known as “Slip-Up of the Yard” in 1974, when he failed to bring the fugitive Great Train Robber, Ronnie Biggs, back to London from Brazil:*

‘I think I have had a very successful assignment to Brazil. My instructions were to trace and detain Ronald Biggs. That is what the assignment was about and I did it. I’m very disappointed not to have brought Biggs back with me, but I’m confident that he will be back in Britain within a few weeks.’

In the Courtroom

Gerald Boyle, *lawyer, opening the case against Jeffrey Dahmer, serial killer who kept his victims heads in the fridge:*

'Ladies and gentlemen of the jury, you are about to embark upon an odyssey.'

William Rees-Davies QC's *opening question to a prosecution witness:*

'Smith, you're a liar, aren't you?'

George Smith, *shouting at Mr Justice Scrutton, summing up in the 'Brides in the Bath' trial:*

'You'll have me hung the way you are going on! Sentence me and have done with it! It's a disgrace to a Christian country, this is! I'm not a murderer, though I may be a bit peculiar!'

Jack Goldenberg, *robber-turned-murderer, to the judge who sentenced him to death:*

'Can I be assured that the thirty-seven pounds found upon me will be declared to be my property.'

Steinie Morrison, *to Mr Justice Darling, who sentenced him to death with the final words 'May God take mercy on your soul':*

'I decline such mercy. I do not believe there is a God in heaven either.'

Frederick Henry Seddon, *as fellow Freemason Mr Justice Bucknill was about to pass sentence on him for murder:*

‘I declare before the Great Architect of the Universe I am not guilty, my lord.’

...questioned about £200 in gold he was said to have counted out an hour after his victim's death:

‘It is a scandalous suggestion – I would have had all day to count the money.’

Charlie Peace *at the Old Bailey, asked by Judge Hawkins, who was about to sentence him for the attempted murder of a policeman, if he had anything to say:*

‘Yes I have this to say, my Lord. I have not been fairly dealt with, and I declare before God that I never had any intention to kill. All I meant to do was frighten him, so I might get away. I really didn't know the pistol was loaded. I hope, my Lord, you will have mercy upon me. I know that I am base and bad. I feel that I am that base and bad, that I am neither fit to live nor die. For I have disgraced myself. I have disgraced my friends and I am not fit to live among mankind. I am not fit to meet my God for I am not prepared to do so. So, oh my Lord, I know I am base and bad to the uttermost, but I know, at the same time, they have painted my case blacker than it really is. I hope you will take all this into consideration and not pass upon me a sentence of imprisonment that will be the means of my dying in prison, where it is possible that I shall not have the chance among my associates to prepare to meet my God that I hope I shall meet. So, my Lord, do have mercy upon me. I beseech you, give me a chance, my Lord, to regain my freedom and you shall not, with the help of my

God, have cause to repent passing a merciful sentence upon me. Oh, my Lord, you yourself expect mercy from the hands of your great and merciful God. Oh, my Lord, do have mercy upon me, a most wretched, miserable man, that man that is not fit to die. I am not fit to live, but with the help of my God I will try to become a good man. I will try to become a man that will be able in the last day to meet my God, my Great Judge, to meet him and to receive the great reward at His hands for my true repentance. So, oh my Lord, have mercy upon me, I pray and beseech you. I will say no more, but, oh my Lord, have mercy upon me. My Lord, have mercy upon me.’

Jae-Kyu Kim, *who assassinated the President of South Korea, to the court martial that sentenced him to death:*

‘As I leave this world I will keep within me this deep gratitude to you all.’

Henry ‘Buller’ Ward, *London villain of the Kray Twins era:*

‘This judge he says to me “Is that what you’re at? Is this your game, going around people’s caffs what’s trying to make a decent living and beating them up?” So I says to him “Don’t be silly, you know I never done it”. And he says “Yes you did. Like it’s been proven with witnesses and that who actually seen you belting him.”’

Chopper Read, *Australian hoodlum who claimed to have been involved in 19 deaths in and out of prison:*

‘There was one case in court where the judge gave me two and a half years and I said: “Two and a half years? How am I going to hold my head up with two and a half years?" I said: "I blew that bloke's leg off. Two and a half years? I'm not leaving here until I get at least three." And the judge said: "You take your two and a half years and be happy with it."'

Trevor Hercules, *villain-turned-author, on a judge who sentenced him:*

'The inevitable half-moon glasses were perched on the end of his nose and his immaculate white wig seemed to be just an extension of the judge himself. I got the feeling that if he took off the wig he would die, and for some reason that wig seemed to be the most important thing in the court. Then a flash of inspiration came to me – it was not Regina the Queen who was the power, it was that nasty wig, kill the wig and you kill the system – I was a genius.'

George Ince, *wrongly accused of the Braintree Barn murder, to Mr Justice Melford Stevenson:*

'I am an Englishman, born and bred in England. This is not an English trial. This is an unfair and biased trial.'

Richard Ramirez, *the Night Stalker, to the judge about to sentence him for thirteen murders, five attempted murders, eleven sexual assaults and fourteen burglaries:*

'I don't believe in the hypocritical, moralistic dogma of this so-called civilised society. I need not look beyond this room to see all the liars, haters, the killers, the crooks, the paranoid cowards – truly trematodes of the Earth, each one in his own legal profession. You maggots make me sick – hypocrites one and all.’

John Henry Seadlund, *American kidnapper and murderer, to the judge who sentenced him to death:*

‘Will I be hanged or fried?’

Aileen Wuornos, *dubbed America's First Serial Killer, to the judge who sentenced her to death:*

‘Thank you. I'll go to heaven now and you will rot in hell.’

Salvatore Santoro, *Mafia underboss, to the judge at his trial:*

‘You're in the driver's seat, your honour, and you're doing a good job. Why don't you give me a hundred years?’

(The judge obliged)

Charles Bronson, *dubbed Britain's most disruptive prisoner, asked how he wished to plead to a charge of taking other prisoners hostage:*

‘As guilty as Adolf Hitler, as guilty as Saddam Hussein.’

...*asked by a judge if he had anything to say after being convicted of taking a hostage in prison:*

‘Just crack on and give me some more porridge.’

(the judge obliged and sentenced him to life imprisonment)

Ned Kelly, *Australian outlaw, on being sentenced to death:*

‘I will return from the grave to fight.’

Charles Becker, *on trial for murder, to his beleaguered attorney:*

‘Between that judge and your inability to stop the D.A., I'm going to fry!’

John Brook, *repeatedly denying the murder of Muriel Patience in the Braintree Restaurant case, to prosecuting counsel:*

‘I'm getting sick of all these "No's". You're wasting the court's time.’

Donald Hume, *to an interpreter whom he addressed as "Buster", referring to the judge in his Swiss trial:*

‘Tell him if it comes to a slanging match I'll rip him to bits verbally as well as I could physically.’

Graham Young, *the St Albans poisoner, accused by the prosecutor at his trial of flippancy:*

‘Since when, Mr Leonard, have poisoners been noted for their absence of humour?’

Gordon Goody, *during the Great Train Robbery trial, to a barrister who passed a sprig of shamrock to him in the dock, on St Patrick's Day:*

‘Thank you very much sir, but I'd rather have bail.’

James Wilkinson, *alleged Wembley Mob bank robber, to a policeman giving evidence at the Old Bailey:*

‘I will swear to Almighty God you are a stinking liar.’

Henry Landru, *French serial killer, to the prosecutor who charged him with eleven murders:*

‘I fully recognise, sir, that you are after my head. I regret that I have not more than one head to offer you.’

. . .asked during the trial about his neighbours complaints of the smell that came from the chimney of his house:

‘Is every smoking chimney and every bad smell proof that a body is being burned?’

. . . shown incriminating notebooks at his trial:

‘Perhaps the police would have preferred to find on page one an entry in these words “I, the undersigned, confess that I have murdered the women whose names are set out herein.”’

...from the dock, to the female spectators who packed his murder trial:

‘I wonder if there is there any lady present who would care to take my seat?’

Horatio Bottomley, *crooked MP, to the Old Bailey jury at his trial on fraud charges:*

‘You will never convict me. The jury is not yet born who would convict me of these charges. (Pointing to the sword of the figure of Justice, above the court) That sword would drop from its scabbard if you gave a verdict of guilty against me.’

(the jury did; the sword didn’t)

Caryl Chessman, *with a shrug, on being sentenced to life imprisonment plus two death sentences:*

‘I still owe 260 years for violating my parole.’

John Haigh, *The Acid Bath Murderer, writing to his parents in 1949 about his forthcoming trial at Lewes Assizes:*

‘I see they are going to run excursions from the South to Lewes next week to see the greatest sensation of the twentieth century. It’s certainly more than they would do for Attlee. Only Princess Margaret or Mr Churchill could command such interest.’

Blackie Audett, *American bank robber and jailbreaker of the 1930s and 40s, on one of his setbacks:*

‘My trial was like the old story about the operation was a success but the patient died. I could prove that the car wasn't stolen but I was found guilty of stealing it anyway.’

Carlos Lehder, *on the injustice of being tried and convicted of drug offences:*

‘I feel like an Indian in a white man's court. Witnesses that never had a second underwear claimed they made millions from Lehder.’

Carl Panzram, *to a jury who had convicted him:*

‘While you were trying me here, I was trying all of you too. I've found you guilty. Some of you I've already executed. If I live, I'll execute some more of you. I hate the whole human race.’

Adolf Hofrichter, *tried in Austria for the murder of a fellow army officer:*

‘The court is a place where little is done with a great deal of noise, a great deal is said, but little justice spoken, and where the individual must pay, whether he will or not.’

John Gotti, *when Judge Leo Glasser threatened to move his trial out of New York:*

‘Where's he going to move it to? Stuttgart, West Germany?

Michele 'The Pope' Greco, *Mafia boss, to the Palermo court that convicted him of thirty two murders:*

‘I wish you peace, tranquillity of spirit. I hope that peace may be with you for the rest of your lives.’

Frank 'The Dasher' Abbandando, *on being convicted of murder and sentenced to death:*

‘I'm gonna miss the first night ball game of the season!’

Charles Manson, *explaining his murderous actions:*

‘I was working at cleaning up my house, something that Nixon should have been doing. He should have been on the side of the road, picking up his children, but he wasn't. He was in the White House, sending them off to war.’

Frederick Deeming, *who claimed to be Jack the Ripper, on trial for murder in a Melbourne court:*

‘If I could believe that I committed the murder I would plead guilty rather than submit to the gaze of the people in this court – the ugliest race of people I have ever seen.’

A**ndrei Chikatilo**, *The Russian Ripper, to the court that found him guilty of fifty five murders and sentenced him to death:*

‘Swindlers! I fought for a free Russia and a free Ukraine. Swindlers!’

Jacques Verges, *controversial French lawyer who represented Klaus Barbie, The Butcher of Lyons:*

‘I wouldn't change my client for all the saints in the world.’

. . . representing Carlos the Jackal, protesting about the way the captured terrorist had been kidnapped in Sudan before being taken to France to face charges:

‘He did not come here on the wings of a swallow.’

Louis Piquett, *John Dillinger's lawyer, asked by a judge why he was seeking a delay in court proceedings:*

‘I've got $40,000 in bonds from the Greencastle robbery, and I'm waiting to fence it to get my fees.’

Clarence Darrow, *renowned Chicago lawyer:*

‘Let Judge Holly speak at my funeral. He knows everything there is to know about me, and he has sense enough not to tell it.’

Ronald Thwaites QC, *telling the jury in the Old Bailey trial of suspected IRA bomber Thomas McAuley that Mr Justice Alliott had not been sleeping when he closed his eyes:*

‘The closed eyes of a judge is the judicial equivalent of telling you our case is a load of rubbish. The judge has been hyper-active throughout the case. He has climbed into the boxing ring time after time and in doing so has not done his job as referee. He has been delivering blows for the prosecution. When he saw Mr McAuley on the ropes it was not the prosecution hitting him below the belt, but the judge himself.’

Desmond de Silva, *lawyer, when the solicitor representing Roderick Newall, who had murdered and buried his parents in Jersey, offered to outline a skeleton argument of the case:*

‘Don't talk to me about skeletons, talk to your client.’

Maitre Carboni, *French lawyer, addressing the jury in the murder trial of Fatalitas Buisson, whose brother Mimile he had earlier failed to save from the guillotine:*

‘Gentlemen, I plead for your indulgence and

clemency. Do not let me have two heads from the same family on my conscience for the rest of my years.’

Richard Rappaport, *an expert witness in the trial of* **John Wayne Gacy***:*

‘Most serial killers will kill with an axe or knife, rather than a gun, in order to achieve intimacy with the victim.’

Unabomber *victim's wife, Susan Mosser, in a Sacramento courtroom, after Theodore Kaczynski had been sentenced to life imprisonment:*

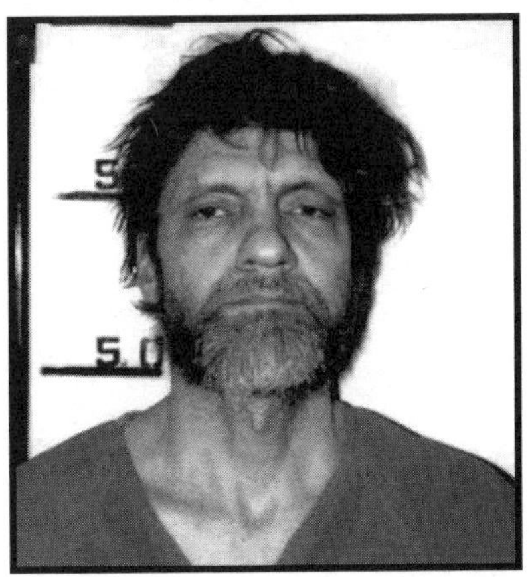

‘Lock him so far down that when he does die, he'll be closer to hell. That is where the devil belongs.’

Reverend Basil Andrews, *asked in the witness box at a 1950s London gangland trial, if he ever told the truth?:*

‘Sometimes’

A witness at the trial of **Jack Henry Abbott***, asked by Abbott if he had read his book* ***In The Belly Of The Beast****:*

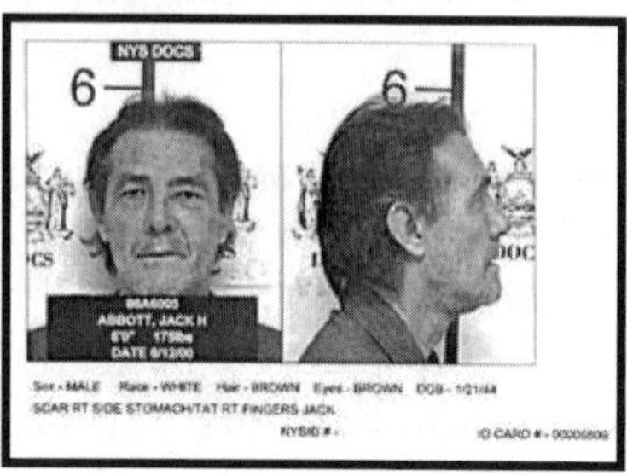

❛I couldn't care less about your books or your thoughts, or anything that is so childish and moronic. You miss the point – it seems to me you are not in the belly of the beast – this is the belly of the beast right here, with guys like you sticking knives in our hearts. You are nothing but a killer.❜

From the Bench...

Mr Justice Melford Stevenson, *sentencing Ronnie Kray to life imprisonment with a recommendation that he serve a minimum of thirty years:*

‘I am not going to waste words on you. In my view society has earned a rest from your activities.’

Mr Justice Edmund Davies, *sentencing the Great Train Robbers to thirty years imprisonment:*

‘Let us clear out of the way any romantic notions of dare-devilry. This is nothing less than a sordid crime of violence inspired by vast greed... To deal with this case leniently would be a positively evil thing. When grave crime is committed it calls for grave punishment, not for the purpose of mere retribution but so that others similarly tempted shall be brought to the sharp realisation that crime does not pay and that the crime is most certainly not worth even the most alluring candle.’

Mr Justice Eveleigh, *jailing former government minister John Stonehouse for fraud and forgery:*

‘You are no ill-fated idealist. In your evidence, you falsely accused people of cant, hypocrisy and humbug - when your defence was all these things.’

Judge Owen Stable, *sentencing three teenage joyriders at Snaresbrook Crown Court in 1994:*

‘If I had a free hand in this country, if it had not sold itself down the river to Europe, and I could sentence you to your just deserts, I would order each one of you to be flogged.’

Lord Cameron, *giving judgement in a Glasgow gang trial in 1978:*

‘The streets of Glasgow are not going to be turned into a ring for ill-conditioned gladiators and their followers.’

. . . rejecting an application from Patrick Meehan's solicitor, for the safecracker, who - as it would later be proved - had been wrongly convicted of murder, to be tested by a truth drug:

‘This Court has a duty to protect an accused person against the folly of his legal advisers.’

Judge Henry Pownall, *halting one of the Brinks Mat laundering trials but refusing to tell the jury the reason:*

‘Believe me, it is a proper reason.’

Mr Justice Goddard, *to the jury in the murder trial of Nurse Dorothea Waddingham, who poisoned her patients:*

‘Can you, as men of common sense, think that anyone in their senses would give a woman suffering from such sharp abdominal pains that morphia had to be given her three nights, two helpings of pork, baked potatoes and fruit pie?’

Lord Denning, *on a civil action brought by the Birmingham Six, before their convictions were eventually overturned:*

‘Just consider the course of events if this action is allowed to proceed to trial. If the six men fail, it will mean that much time and money will have been expended by many people for no good purpose. If the six men win, it will mean that the police were guilty of perjury, that they were guilty of violence and threats, that the confessions were involuntary and were improperly admitted in evidence and that the convictions were erroneous. That would mean the Home Secretary would either have to recommend they be pardoned or he would have to remit the case to the Court of Appeal. This is such an appalling vista that every sensible person in the land would say: "It cannot be right these actions should go any further."

This case shows what a civilised country we are. Here are six men who have been proved guilty of the most wicked murder of twenty-one innocent people. They have no money. Yet the state has lavished large sums on their defence. They were convicted of murder and sentenced to imprisonment for life. In their evidence they were guilty of gross perjury. Yet the state continued to lavish large sums on them in actions against the police. It is high time it stopped. It is really an attempt to set aside the convictions on a side wind. It is a scandal that it should be allowed to continue.'

Mr Justice Laws, *to Mike Mansfield QC, as the latter emphasised a point in court:*

'Do not wag your finger at me, Mr Mansfield. I will listen just as carefully without it.'

Mr Justice Leonard, *to Helena Kennedy QC:*

'I am not the jury – please don't harangue me.'

Judge Edward D. Cowart, *to mass murderer Ted Bundy:*

‘You'd have made a good lawyer. I'd have loved to have you practise in front of me.’

Mr Justice Avory, *hearing in the appeal of Major Herbert Armstrong, convicted of poisoning his wife:*

‘To find a packet of three and a half grains of white arsenic in a solicitor's pocket is surely rare.’

Mr Justice Scrutton, *summing up in the trial of George Smith, the Brides in the Bath murderer in 1915:*

‘Since last August, all over Europe, thousands of lives of combatants, sometimes of non-combatants, have been taken daily, with no warning and in many cases with no justification...And yet, while this wholesale destruction of human life is going on, for some days all the apparatus of justice in England has been considering whether the prosecution are right in saying that one man should die.’

Mr Justice Bean, *sentencing Marty Frape for his part in the Parkhurst Prison riot of 1969:*

‘My tragedy and your tragedy is that I must protect society from the wildness of your ravings.’

Judge Michael Argyle, *at the Old Bailey, freeing a defendant charged with attempted rape of a model:*

‘You come from Derby, which is my part of the country. Now off you go and don't come back.’

A Rochdale magistrate *to John Ellis, former hangman who tried to commit suicide by shooting himself – but succeeded in only fracturing his jaw:*

‘If your aim had been as true as the drops you have given it would have been a bad job for you.’

Mr Justice Devlin, *to a Manchester jury in the trial of Renee Duffy, charged with the murder of her husband:*

❛What matters is whether this girl had time to say "Whatever I have suffered, whatever I have endured, I know that: Thou shalt not kill."❜

Judge Ian Starforth Hill, *to a car thief, arrested after a 100 mph chase through Farnborough:*

❛It is a thousand pities you didn't damage yourself.❜

Lord Chief Justice Parker, *summing up in the trial of the war-time atom spies, Alan Nunn May and Klaus Fuchs:*

❛This has been a case, which, by its very nature has been full of intrigue. You may say it has the characteristics of what is called a thriller.❜

Judge Lynne Abrahams *of Philadelphia, sentencing serial killer Gary Heidnik to 120 years imprisonment:*

❛I don't want any parole order to put Mr Heidnik back on the streets as long as he's breathing.❜

Judge H. Lyle, *once Al Capone's lawyer, speaking of his former client:*

❛We'll send him to the chair if possible. He deserves to die and has no right to live. Capone has become an almost mythical being. He is not a myth, but a reptile who deserves to be crushed.❜

Judge Samuel Conti, *frustrated by the legal manoeuvrings of three hundred defence attorneys in a San Francisco Hells Angels' case:*

❛I'd like to get this case over with in my lifetime.❜

Judge Samuel Leibowitz, *to Vito Genovese, after a jury had acquitted him of murder:*

Last photograph of Vito Genovese – in prison where he died

'I cannot speak for the jury, but I believe that if there were even a shred of corroborating evidence you would have been condemned to the electric chair. By devious means, among which were the terrorising of witnesses, kidnapping them, yes, even murdering those who would give evidence against you, you have thwarted justice time and again.'

Credit Where It's Due

Jack Ruby, *to an Assistant D.A, following his arrest for shooting Lee Harvey Oswald:*

'Well, you guys couldn't do it. Somebody had to do it. That son of a bitch killed my President.'

Edward Bunker, *ex-convict and Mr Blue in Reservoir Dogs:*

'San Quentin's doctors are the world's best with knife wounds.'

Fat Tony Salerno, *head of the Genovese Mafia family, taped by undercover police:*

'If it wasn't for me there wouldn't be no mob left. I made all the guys. And everybody's a good guy.'

John Barrett, *mafioso, complaining about his boss, Meyer Lansky:*

'It ain't fair. We take all the risks and he gets all the gravy.'

Ned Kelly, *Australian outlaw, hanged in Melbourne in 1880:*

'Had I robbed, plundered, ravished and murdered everything I met, my character could not be painted blacker than it is at present, but, thank God, my conscience is as clear as the snow in Peru.'

Charlie Lowe, *supergrass, questioned about a conspiracy involving stolen cheques:*

‘Coshing people and robbing them is more my game, sir, not cheques.’

Renalto Aguda, *convicted armed robber:*

‘Having been to prison, I am a better Freemason for it, because I have been at the other end of the Nine O'Clock Toast.’

Wladyslaw Mazurkiewicz, *Polish serial killer, on allegations that he had killed up to fifty times:*

‘People are crediting me with too much. I planned only eight murders, I want the record put right.’

Arthur Hutchinson, *on trial for rape and murder, asked if he regarded himself as attractive to women:*

‘I haven't had many complaints.’

Sir William Waterlow, *printer of banknotes and postage stamps, after being deceived by a false passport presented by swindler, Karl Marang:*

‘I'm a printer, not a detective.’

Mad Frankie Fraser:

‘The Independent had it wrong when their reporter said I'd been shot dead outside Turnmills Night Club in 1991. I was only in hospital for two days that time.’

Donald Hume, *charged with murder in a Swiss court:*

‘It is very likely a strange thing to come from me, but I have a conscience. It is only a little one, but it is there.’

Arnold Rothstein, *known as "The Big Bankroll":*

❛You want to know how I make money? There are two million fools born for every intelligent man. That ought to answer you.❜

...speaking to author, Damon Runyon, about his gambling house:

❛People like to think they're better than other people. As long as they're willing to pay to prove it, I'm willing to let them.❜

Carlos Lehder, *much-sought Columbian drug baron, to William Lemas, the FBI agent who arrested him.*

❛Oh, little chief. What a hot number you are. You're the most famous man in the world. You know those gringo sons of bitches want to hang me by the balls and now you've got me. Too bad we didn't meet earlier.❜

Nina Housden, *who strangled her husband with a washing line in a fit of irrational jealousy:*

❛Charlie wasn't a bad egg. He just made the mistake of running around with other women.❜

Serge Rubinstein's wife, *who had divorced him for knocking her unconscious and ripping off her clothes, speaking after the Russian-born swindler's death:*

‘He was very kind.’

Tony Wild, *supergrass:*

‘I've generally found that villains – I don't mean pickpockets and burglars – but villains, are very pleasant company. Gentlemen, a lot of them.’

Arthur Harding, *East End villain of the early 1900s:*

‘Arthur Phale was my solicitor. He was a crooked solicitor, that is you could trust him. Any villainery, he'd do it for you.’

Jabez Balfour, *Victorian fraudster, recalled by a former servant:*

‘I thought of him then as a great gentleman. He was ugly and fat, you know, with a thin little beard but he had glittering eyes.’

John McVicar, *on Jimmy Moody, London robber who escaped from Brixton Prison in 1980 and remained on the run until he was shot dead in a pub thirteen years later:*

‘Never MENSA material, he made up for it by growling at everybody. He was the sort of person who could be walking down the middle of the Sahara Desert and still be odds-on to cause a row – even if it was with himself.’

Graham Young, *the St. Albans Poisoner, on hearing at the age of fourteen that doctors had diagnosed his father as suffering from arsenic poisoning:*

‘How ridiculous! Fancy not knowing how to tell the difference between antimony and arsenic poisoning.’

Sir Edward Henry, *Commissioner of the Metropolitan Police in 1912, asking an Old Bailey judge to be merciful to Alfred Bowes, who had shot and wounded him:*

‘He was ambitious to become a taxi-driver. All ambition is a good thing and I would not wish him to suffer unduly because of that ambition.’

Eddie Guerin, *on the legend that surrounded his much-publicised escape from Devil's Island:*

‘What I am about to narrate now is nothing but the plain unadulterated truth. The time has come when I can tell it, if only for the purpose of finally killing the preposterous stories that were put into circulation when I made my escape from the penal settlement in French Guiana. The wild lying that went on! It was alleged that three of us had got away from Devil's Island in a boat and that one of the party had been killed and eaten to keep the remaining two of us alive! I know I have been many things in my time, but I have not yet been reduced to the straits when I could be compelled to turn cannibal.’

Victor Meek, *policeman-cum-author:*

‘I enjoyed every arrest I ever made, from simple drunks to life-sentence felons. The high-speed chases on wet, dark nights, the squealing tyres, the final tipping-over of a stolen car, the pursuit of a survivor across the fields, with stick out and shouting threats and curses till their hearts failed them and they stopped; these I loved. But I seldom loved the prisoners. Their essential stupidity irritated me, particularly the “clever” ones. In return they showed me their affection by giving me nicknames such as Black Jack, Snatcher and Old Bastard-face.’

Martin Cahill, *'The General' of the Irish underworld, blaming his criminality on the teachers at the reform school he was sent to as a youth:*

‘If anyone corrupted me, it was those mad monks down in the bog.’

Tony Lambrianou, *former member of the Kray Firm, in 1991:*

‘I've protected the Krays for years, but I got nothing in return.’

Charles Sobraj, *Vietnamese drug dealer, robber and murderer:*

‘I consider myself a businessman, not a criminal. And I never killed good people.’

Cynthia Payne:

‘If I am to be remembered for anything, I would like it to be for having run a really nice brothel and providing a social need.’

...on men:

‘The trouble with men is that for a woman to have a civilized conversation with them they need despunking first.’

Professor Valery Fabricant, *who shot dead four colleagues at Montreal University:*

‘Either I am insane, in which case everything is OK; but, if a normal person shot four people, questions have to be asked and the answers are terrifying.’

Edward Bunker, *on his experience in dealing with authority:*

‘If there was a God of Justice, I am unsure what would happen if He put what I did on one end of the scale and what was done to me on the other.’

Carl Panzram, *serial killer:*

‘I would not reform if the front gate was opened right now and if I was given a million dollars when I stepped out. I have no desire to do good or to be good.’

Lawrence Mangano, *who was arrested 200 times but never spent a day in jail.*

‘They were all bum raps. And besides, I had good lawyers.’

Ted Bundy, *to his biographers:*

‘I don't care what you write, just so you get it right and just so it sells.’

Denis Nilsen, *to a documentary film crew visiting him in Albany Prison:*

‘I don't want to look like a bloody monster, I want to look interesting. Make me look interesting.’

...on the public's interest in crimes such as his own:

‘I am always surprised and truly amazed that anyone can be attracted by the macabre. The population at large is neither "ordinary" nor "normal". They seem to be bound together by a collective ignorance of what they are. They have, every one of them, got their deep, dark thoughts, with many a skeleton rattling in their secret cupboards.’

Al Capone:

‘I’m no angel. I’m not posing as a model for youth. I’ve had to do a lot of things I didn’t like to do. But I’m not as black as I’m painted. I’m human. I’ve got a heart in me. I’ll go as deep in my pocket as any man to help any guy that needs help. I can’t stand to see anybody hungry or cold or helpless. Many a poor family in Chicago thinks I’m Santa Claus.’

...asked what a man thought as he killed another in gang wars:

‘Well, maybe he thinks that the law of self-defence, the way God looks at it, is a little broader than the law books have it...Maybe it means killing a man who’d kill you if he saw you first. Maybe it means killing a man in defence of your business – the way you make your money to take care of your wife and child. I think it does. You can’t blame me for thinking there’s worse fellows in the word than me.’

...on supplying bootleg liquor during the Prohibition years:

‘All I ever did was to sell beer to our finest people. All I ever did was to supply a demand that was pretty popular. Why, the very guys that make my trade good are the ones that yell loudest about me. Some of the leading judges use the stuff.’

George Smithson, *country house burglar of the 1920s:*

‘Throughout the whole of my criminal career nothing has astounded me more than the kindly, generous way I have been treated by people whom I have robbed. I fully expected, after I had been captured in April 1923, and was being asked to account for booty worth many thousands of pounds, that I would have a rough time at the hands of the unfortunate individuals whose places had been despoiled. Precisely the reverse was the case, though I am not putting the treatment I received as an inducement for any other budding crook to take up a life of crime.'

'...The average dog is a humbug when it comes to guarding property. I have broken into hundreds of houses and never been attacked by one yet. It may be, of course, that I had some sort of mesmeric influence over them, but I can honestly say without the slightest hesitation that they are a joke to a competent burglar.'

F.Lee Bailey, *lawyer, explaining why his client, better known as The Boston Strangler, had evaded detection for so long:*

'After knowing Albert De Salvo for half an hour, the average person would feel perfectly comfortable about inviting him home for dinner to meet the family.'

'...I don't think De Salvo is dangerous, but I'm not about to bet my reputation or my wife's life on it.'

Horatio Bottomley, *crooked M.P. after giving evidence at Westminster Magistrates Court:*

'What a nice old gentleman on the bench. He let me say what I liked. I think I shall retain him to hear all my future cases!'

John Hamilton *of the Dillinger Gang, described by his girlfriend after her arrest:*

❛He acted like a gentleman. Why, I never heard him say "damn". And clean! He'd take two baths a day.❜

A Sicilian Police Commissioner *recalling the generosity of Mafia don, Luciano Leggio:*

❛He wasn't just rich himself. Everybody who worked for him, covered for him, sheltered him, nursed him, was rich. The source of his power from the start was that fatal, lightning readiness to kill. But in the end it was money too. The man gushed money.❜

Paul Castellano, *Mafia Boss of Bosses, described by an FBI agent:*

❛He is the best-insulated son of a bitch I've ever seen in my life.❜

An Irish Garda, *seeing Martin Cahill - "The General" – wearing a ski mask to avoid being recognised:*

❛There's nothing wrong in that. He's an ugly-looking fucker.❜

Carmine Galante, *described by a New York police chief:*

❛I used to say the rest of them were copper, but he was pure steel. When he spoke, he made others shudder.❜

Joe Valachi, *on the panic which ensued when four police officers were spotted close to the 1957 Apalachin Conference of Mafia leaders:*

❛There they are, running through the woods like rabbits, throwing away money so they won't be caught with a lot of cash, and some of them throwing away guns. So who are they kidding when they say we got to respect them?'

George 'Bugs' Moran, *asked by a reporter who he thought was responsible for the St Valentine's Day massacre:*

'Only Capone kills like that!'

J.Edgar Hoover, *taken to task for referring to John Dillinger as "a rat" in a speech:*

'Well, wasn't he a rat? Wasn't he everything that was low and vile? Didn't he hide behind women? Didn't he shoot from ambush? Wasn't his whole career as filthy as that of any rat that ever lived?'

describing Alvin Karpis, bank robber:

'He seems old in spite of his comparative youth. His eyes are aged, penetrating and rodent-like, as if they had looked forever from dark corners. His mouth is the most cruelly thin slice I have ever seen. His cheeks are those of an old, thin man, which have drooped and jowled until they can be described only as slab-like. His language is so foul that it seems impossible for anyone to have learned so many blasphemous invectives.'

Mandy Rice-Davies, *fifteen years after the death of her ex-lover, the notorious property racketeer Peter Rachman:*

‘I often think of Peter, even today. He taught me such a lot – right down to little things – like how to roll a pair of socks properly.’

Chief Inspector Walter Dew, *the policeman who arrested Dr Crippen on board the SS Montrose and charged him with the murder and mutilation of his wife, Belle Elmore:*

‘There was something almost likeable about the mild little fellow who squinted through thick-lensed spectacles, and whose sandy mustache was out of all proportion to his build.’

Trevor Burke, QC, *on how watching the movie* ***To Kill A Mockingbird*** *with his mother, when he was twelve, inspired him to become a barrister:*

‘She watched Gregory Peck as the lawyer and said “You look like Gregory Peck and you could do that, son” and I thought she’s right, I could.’

Edmund Burke, *18th Century MP, to the House of Commons:*

‘The justices of Middlesex are generally the scum of the earth: carpenters, brick-makers and shoe-makers, some of whom are notoriously men of infamous character that they are unworthy of any employ whatsoever, and others so ignorant that they can scarcely write their own names.’

Jack Henry Abbott, *described by the prosecutor at his trial for the murder of Richard Adan:*

‘This is a killer – a killer by habit, a killer by inclination, a killer by philosophy and a killer by desire.’

John Bindon's *obituary in The Independent:*

❛He was a genial fellow, welcome everywhere he went, from the highest to the lowest places. He could make a horse laugh.❜

Charlie Richardson *on his associate, Mad Frankie Fraser:*

❛Frankie has done more for penal reform than the whole bloody Howard League for Penal Reform. He fights the system to improve it for other prisoners.They put him up as "Mad" Frank but really he's too sane.❜

Emmett Dalton, *last of the notorious Dalton brothers, writing in 1931 of the hypocritical way society regards its criminals:*

❛The kid-glove bandit, a courtly figment of popular fancy, is the current fashion in outlaws. He is almost enshrined in our national gallery of hero types. With scarce secret complaisance we thrill at his maraudings - until he sticks a gun under our nose. Then he becomes a dastardly villain.❜

Joe Bonanno, *Mafia Godfather, on a Family feud:*

❛To trace the origins of the Castellammarese War, one has to bring on stage Al Capone, the Neapolitan whose surname, in Italian, means a castrated male chicken.❜

Sir James Paget, *royal surgeon and joint founder of pathology, after the trial of Adelaide Bartlett, who poisoned her husband without leaving any traces:*

❛Now that she has been quite properly acquitted she should, in the interests of science, tell us how she did it.❜

Patrick Meehan, *Glasgow safecracker:*

‘Children from a slum area are called juvenile delinquents and are sent to approved schools. Children from a middle-class area are called naughty and sent home.’

Peter Scott:

‘The word cat-burglar has been romanticised. You’re really only a dishonest window cleaner. I watch window cleaners doing much more dangerous things than I’ve ever done.’

Terry Druggan, *of the Chicago Valley Gang, waving his gun at Jewish gangsters whose truckload of beer he had just hi-jacked, and pointing to a nearby church:*

‘Hats off, you Jews, when you’re passing the house of God, or I’ll shoot them off.’

Albert De Salvo, *The Boston Strangler:*

‘The poor always get punished. That’s the way the world is. Rich people can do all kinds of sex things and get away with it. They just buy their way out.’

Joseph Columbo, *Mafia boss, on the FBI:*

‘The greatest organisation in the country – except when they’re framing our children and harassing our pregnant women.’

Frank Costello, *known in Mafia circles as ‘The Prime Minister’, to a newspaperman:*

‘If you say that I am a gambler you will be right. But I am an uncommon gambler. An uncommon gambler is a man who accommodates common gamblers.’

Jim Moody, *FBI man on the difference between the American and Russian mafias:*

‘John Gotti doesn’t have college-educated people and trained military officers like the Russian mafia does.’

Carlos Lehder, *on how the drug trade helped the Columbian economy:*

‘That was our obligation, to bring dollars back to our people however we could. It can be called Mafia, it can be called syndicate, it can be called a bonanza, it can be called whatever you like.’

Herman Drenth, *who admitted five murders but was believed to have committed many more in his home made gas chamber:*

‘You’ve got me now on five, what good would fifty more do?’

Reverend J. Frank Norris, *pastor of the First Baptist Church in Fort Worth, Texas, who shot and killed a parishioner for complaining about his pulpit manner:*

‘Should the Devil have all the best tunes? Should Beelzebub have all the applause? Why shouldn’t people applaud in church? It proves that they are alive. What’s the difference between a lot of deacons and preachers in the Amen corner shouting their “Amens” and allowing the congregation to express their “Amens” by clapping their hands?

...They don’t like my sensational methods. They want a nice quiet mealy-mouthed preacher who hasn’t the guts to hit sin hard and fight the gang. Join my church. We’ve got a great fight on here now. But we’ve got the enemy on the run. They’re licked but they’re still kicking.

They talk about dignity and solemnity. Poppycock! Too many preachers think that a church should be like a graveyard. By all means, go to the graveyard if you want dignity and solemnity. I prefer life! Sensation is life! lack of sensation is stagnation! A lot of preachers are so dignified they are petrified.
...J.Frank Norris will never preach to empty benches. I'll have a crowd if I have to start a dog fight.'

Lee Harvey Oswald, *following his arrest on suspicion of shooting President John F. Kennedy:*

'I have read the Bible. It is fair reading but not very interesting. As a matter of fact, I am a student of philosophy.'

Feds and Cops

John MacLean, *Glasgow policeman, on his former Chief Constable Percy Sillitoe:*

‘He got together the biggest and hardest men in the force, and ordered them to go out and batter the living shite out of every Ned who scratched his balls without permission. I'm telling you we didn't have to be asked twice.’

Gene Radano, *former American policeman, on those who would criticise the police:*

‘How many of those college-graduate citizens – who do all the squawking about humanity – how many of them ever had to deal with a mob? They never even heard what a mob sounds like! Yet they want to sit and judge us! Everybody wants to judge us these days! And they'll judge you too when the time comes. What the hell do they know about a mob? No bastard knows anything except the poor cop whose ass is on the line. A mob is the ugliest animal in the world! You just try to quiet them by quoting something out of a book. They'd run over you like a herd of cattle! And you haven't got time to wait for the Supreme Court to make a decision You only got five seconds to decide whether to run like a dog or stand up like a cop. Five seconds: you, God, a mob and no reference books. So you hold the club short and you hit the first son-of-a-bitch on the head – bang! three stitches! If the bastard keeps coming – bang! three more stitches! And that makes you a fascist! For weeks they'll argue whether you did or didn't use too much force! For weeks! And you only had five seconds! I say the cop who stands up for law and order does more than a roomful of judges.'

William O'Connor, *Chief Detective of Chicago, addressing his force in 1928:*

'Men, the war is on. We have got to show that society and the police department, and not a bunch of dirty rats, are running this town. It is the wish of the people of Chicago that you hunt these criminals down and kill them without mercy. Your cars are equipped with machine guns and you will meet the enemies of society on equal terms. See to it that they do not have you pushing up daisies. Make them push up daisies. Shoot first and shoot to kill. If you kill a notorious feudist you will get a handsome reward and win promotion. If you meet a car containing bandits, pursue them and fire. When I arrive on the scene my hopes will be fulfilled if you have shot off the top of the car and killed every criminal inside it.'

Morgan A. Collins, *Chicago police chief, in 1926:*

'I don't want to encourage the business, but if somebody has to be killed, it's a good thing the gangsters are murdering themselves off. It saves trouble for the police.'

Raul Diaz, *of the Miami Homicide Squad, on targeting suspects:*

‘We weren’t going to violate their constitutional rights, but they were either going to die, go to jail or leave Florida.’

Detective Sergeant Harold Challenor, *‘bent copper’, on crime in London in the 1950s and early 60s:*

‘Fighting crime in Soho was like trying to swim against a tide of sewage; you made two strokes forward and were swept back three. For every villain you put behind bars there were always two more to take their place. Most of them were professional crooks and if there is any truth in the cliché crime doesn’t pay they never got the message.’

‘*...on meeting a man in court whom he had earlier planted evidence upon:*

‘I did not recognise Rooum and went up and said “Wotcher, me old darling, what about playing football for us on Sunday?”’

‘...A truncheon is not for rolling out the pastry. It is designed to hit people.’

Victor Meek, *policeman-cum-author, on police communications:*

‘I believe that three short, sharp blasts on the whistle have considerable value. Windows go up and witnesses result. Those few policemen who hear the faint sound of the flute either say “That kid wants his ear clipped, that sounds just like a police flute” and go serenely on their way, or they run towards it, often in my experience blowing their own, so that those who hear the latter run in that direction rather than the original one.’

Nipper Read, *Scotland Yard detective, famous for arresting the Krays:*

‘A good villain expects to be followed. He will go down the Tube, turn and come out again, get on a train and get out of the doors as they close, take a bus and drop off at traffic lights, go in a store with a number of exits by one door and leave by a different one. Suddenly he will jump into a cab. In a pub he will leave his drink and go to the lavatory. Five minutes later you realise there is an exit into another bar. He is following his profession and self-preservation comes high on the list of his priorities.’

...on the lack of well-known detectives today:

‘There was one detective who retired some months ago and it was said he had investigated more murders than anyone else. I thought – who is he? Everyone in the country should know who he is and what he’s achieved.’

Nutty Sharpe:

‘On the day I retired as Chief of the Flying Squad I read how crooks spat on the ground when I walked by – hooey. Every time I stroll through Piccadilly, Leicester Square and neighbourhood I get more handshakes from crooks and ex-crooks than from any other class of people.’

...revealing a curious affection for the villains he was employed to chase:

‘They’re a colourful, rascally lot, these wide ‘uns, but they are human and often kind and almost invariably they are humorous and entertaining.’

Jack Slipper - *Slipper of the Yard - explaining how the police investigating the Great Train Robbery overlooked £140,000 hidden in Ronnie Biggs' coal shed:*

‘The officers couldn't really be blamed. Unless you've had a whisper from a good snout – something like “He's got money and he's blackened his hands” – you wouldn't be too eager to move half a ton of coal.’

Sir Robert Mark, *on what he found when he took over as Metropolitan Police Commissioner:*

‘I had never experienced institutionalised wrongdoing, blindness, arrogance and prejudice on anything like the scale accepted as routine in the Met.’

Superintendent Tony Lundy, *on doing his job in the early 1980s, while suspected of corruption:*

‘I was being investigated from pillar to post, but for three years I seemed to be living at the Old Bailey. I had six courts running at one stage. I was getting out of one witness box, jumping into another one, out of that into another, days at a time. And the same defence barristers kept strapping me. I was investigating murders half the time, and I was the victim of attempted murder - character assassination – for the other half.’

Police Superintendent Walter Cowman, *on the case of Samuel Perera, who killed and dissected his adopted daughter in 1983:*

‘I don't think I shall ever forget the sight of a virtually complete human spine curled around the roots of a plant.’

Peter Bleksley, *former Scotland Yard undercover detective:*

❛I think a lot of informants assume that because you are playing the part of a villain, you must be a bit of a villain. The better the undercover guy is, the more likely he is to find himself being offered dodgy dealings. They think you really are one of them, not just Plod playing the bad guy.❜

...on the personal price he paid:

❛My CV should have read "Professional liar, Metropolitan Police, treachery my speciality. Available for all kinds of undercover operations." Perhaps it should have added, "Prepared to sacrifice home life, domestic life, all friends and family and mingle freely with then dregs of society in the pursuit of duty."❜

Bill Sharp, *a Metropolitan police officer, writing in Police Review, about a call for greater fitness among policemen:*

❛Where do you think you're going to find these supermen – policemen from 18 to 60 who can, while wearing full uniform, raincoat, boots, handcuffs, personal radio, truncheon etc., outrun a 15 year old, outbox the local ABA champion, climb mountains and swim the Channel?❜

John Alderson, *former Chief Constable, on arming the British police:*

❛If you police an armed society, you learn to shoot first or you're dead.❜

❛...If a New York cop was on duty in London, he would be in jail within a week; if a London bobby was on duty in New York, he would be dead within a week.❜

Paul Condon, *Metropolitan Police Commissioner, on TV in 1993:*

‘The combination of drugs, money, firearms and ruthless criminals is very dangerous.’

J. Edgar Hoover, *as head of the FBI, denying the existence of the Mafia to Attorney General, Robert Kennedy in 1962:*

‘No single individual or coalition of racketeers dominates organised crime across the country.’

...to Mafia boss Frank Costello, who tried to strike up conversation with him in a barbershop:

‘You stay out of my bailiwick and I'll stay out of yours.’

...on his right to speak his mind:

‘I'm going to tell the truth about these rats. I'm going to tell the truth about their dirty, filthy, diseased women. I'm going to tell the truth about the miserable politicians who protect them and the slimy, silly or sob-sister convict lovers who let them out on sentimental or ill-advised paroles. If the people don't like it they can get me fired. But I'm going to say it.’

...asked in retirement what was the greatest thrill of his career:

‘The night we got John Dillinger.’

Eliot Ness *of The Untouchables, recalled by Chicago reporter, Jack McPhaul:*

‘Ness was an honest man. That was his claim to fame. That's why they called him the Untouchable. But he never fired a shot in anger and nobody ever shot at him. When he and his fellas went to raid a brewery the owners just went out the back door. They weren't going to shoot a federal man, it wasn't worth it.

They could start an operation somewhere else. I knew Ness in Chicago and also years later when he was commissioner of public safety in Cleveland. He never lived to see his book published...but when the TV people purchased the rights all they kept was the title. In the series he was constantly shooting it out with Capone but in real life he had no dealings with him.’

Giovanni Falcone, *anti-Mafia prosecutor:*

‘Investigating the Mafia is like crossing minefields: never take a step before making sure that you are not going to put your foot on an anti-personnel mine. This principle is valid for all investigations that deal with organised crime, but all the more so for someone like me, for I was venturing into what was virtually virgin territory under crossfire from friends and enemies alike, even within the magistrature.’

Charlie Peace, *Victorian burglar and murderer:*

‘The police never think of suspecting anyone who wears good clothes.’

Martin Cahill, *'The General' of the Irish underworld until his death in 1994, on the police:*

‘You must never, ever look at them. Their presence must never be acknowledged.’

...taunting the police for their inability to capture and convict him.

‘Since they go everywhere we go, we can offer an armed gardai escort for the movement of large amounts of cash.’

Billy Hill, *self-styled Boss of Britain's Underworld, on a police raid at premises containing 20,000 toys in cardboard boxes, rather than the bullion they sought:*

‘They were swarming in dozens in the warehouse, opening every box and closely examining every talking doll and teddy bear. As they held up the dolls to look at them they murmured "Aah" and as they turned over the teddy bears they grunted "Ooh". In the end the place sounded like a blinking zoo with all the "oohs" and "aahs".’

Jimmy Boyle:

‘One of the fears one has when being charged by detectives is that they are prone to writing down what they think you should be saying rather than what you are actually saying. This is called verballing.’

Tony Mancini, *who confessed to a newspaper that he was guilty of the Brighton Trunk Murder, for which he had been acquitted:*

‘Where the police are concerned, a man who's got convictions never gets a square deal.’

Harry Roberts, *the Shepherds Bush police killer:*

‘We were professional criminals. we don't react the same way as ordinary people. The police aren't like real people to us.’

Mad Frankie Fraser:

‘There's always something good about seeing a copper go down. The trouble is it doesn't happen often enough.’

Buster Edwards, *Great Train Robber:*

‘I’ve not got much time for Old Bill but I feel sorry for them with all these violent crimes.’

Arthur Harding, *London villain of the early 1900s, on the murder of a policeman in Houndsditch:*

‘I had a great respect for those people who killed the policeman even though I don’t believe in killing policemen.’

Kenneth Noye, *Brinks Mat gold launderer, on being told that the man he had stabbed to death in his garden was undercover policeman, John Fordham:*

‘Old Bill no, he had no business being here.’

Ned Kelly, *expressing a dislike of Australian policemen:*

‘What would people say if they saw a strapping big lump of an Irishman shepherding sheep for fifteen bob a week or tailing turkeys in Tallarook ranges for a smile from Julia or even begging his tucker, they would say he ought to be ashamed of himself and tar-and-feather him. But he would be a king to a policeman who for a lazy loafing cowardly billit left the ash corner deserted for shamrock, the emblem of true wit and beauty to serve under a flag and nation that has destroyed, massacreed and murdered their forefathers by the greatest torture as rolling them downhill in spiked barrels, pulling their toe and finger nails on the wheel and every torture imaginable.’

‘Big, ugly, fat-necked, wombat-headed, big-bellied, magpie-legged, narrow-hipped, splay-footed sons of Irish bailiffs or English landlords, which is better known as officers of justice or Victoria Police.’

John Dillinger, *to Tucson police who had arrested him:*

‘We’re exactly like you cops. You have a profession – we have a profession. Only difference is, you’re on the right side of the law, we’re on the wrong.’

Danny Ahearn, *New York bootlegger, on the police:*

‘They got to make a buck. They’re human too. Treat ‘em nice. Then if you get into trouble you may be able to do business with ’em.’

Albert Spaggiari, *French bank robber:*

‘Crooks, like people in finance or entertainment, transact their business via phone and telex. They travel by jet and use computers to do their bookkeeping, whereas most cops still have to count on their fingers.’

The Zodiac Killer, *in a letter to the Los Angeles Times in 1971:*

‘If the blue menaces are ever going to catch me, they had better get off their fat butts and do something.’

Peter Sutcliffe, *The Yorkshire Ripper, on the bungled police hunt for him:*

‘It was miracle that they didn’t apprehend me earlier. They had all the facts. They knew it was me.’

Rosario Borgio, *Ohio Mafia don, to his men, declaring war on police who had raided his whorehouses and gambling dens:*

‘I want you to kill every cop in Akron. You got that? Every cop out there in the city. Now, right now! Two hundred and fifty dollars a head for policemen! You kill a cop I give you two hundred and fifty dollars, right away. Just make sure you kill him, not just hurt him. He never gets up again. Dead. All of them, dead.’

Abe ‘Kid Twist’ Reles, *Murder Inc. hitman, on trial:*

‘I will take on any cop in the city with pistols, fists or anything else. A cop counts to fifteen when he puts his finger on the trigger before he shoots.’

David Berkowitz, *‘Son of Sam’, on his trail of murder:*

‘The demons were protecting me. I had nothing to fear from the police.’

The Jailhouse

John Dillinger:

‘A jail is just like a nut with a worm in it. The worm can always get out.’

... arriving at Pendleton Reformatory for his first prison sentence:

‘I won’t cause you any trouble except to escape. I can beat your institution.’

Walter ‘Angel Face’ Probyn, *on the reluctance of prisoners to escape from Dartmoor:*

‘What I found out was that all these hardened criminals were petrified of the dark. I had a brother-in-law there who used to go around putting the cosh about and snatching money bags, really doing damage to people, a big, hard thug – he wouldn’t escape from Dartmoor because he was frightened of the sheep and the cows and the darkness. He nearly tore my bollocks off one day going over a barbed-wire fence. Some cows appeared and he grabbed hold of me in fear and tried to pull himself over while I was straddled over a barbed wire fence. It was just a cow with great udders.’

Alfred Hinds, *celebrated jailbreaker of the 1950s and 60s:*

‘Escape is one of the great prison topics but few prisoners ever get beyond discussing it. In fact most of them don't really need to be locked in at all. Prison security is often ridiculously exaggerated. I've seen old men of eighty on sticks in a maximum security prison like Parkhurst. The vast majority of prisoners are resigned if not content to do their bird.'

Dave Courtney, *London TV-villain-turned author:*

'You could fill in a form and apply for books from an outside library. So I put down The Great Escape, The Life of Houdini and Tunnel Diggers Monthly. Didn't hear a dicky bird.'

George Blake, *Soviet spy serving forty two years, who escaped from Wormwood Scrubs in 1996:*

'It was clear to me from the very beginning that if I wanted to escape I had first of all to create the firm impression all round that I had no intention of doing so.'

Illich Ramirez Sanchez – *Carlos the Jackal – to his controversial lawyer, Jacques Verges, visiting him in a Paris prison:*

'I will be out of here pretty soon and I believe you may well be taking my place. I promise to leave you a clean cell.'

Jimmy Boyle:

'The fact is that prison eats your insides out and ties your stomach in knots, leaving your heart very heavy. All of this takes place when you are alone, but it wouldn't be the done thing to let this be seen by other people.'

Charles Sobraj, *Vietnamese mass murderer and prison escaper, speaking of his captors:*

‘Always remember that their desire to keep me locked up is no match for my desire to be free.’

Mafalda Capone, *incredulous that her brother Al had been sent to jail:*

‘He never gets in jail. What would he want to go to jail for? That's one place he never had a desire to go. He liked to talk of Europe, of Palm Beach, of the famous race tracks, of the scenes at the big fight – but jail – oh no, not for Al.’

Herby Sperling, *American mobster who was sentenced to life without parole for his role as New York link to the French Connection, on modern-day prison conditions:*

‘They give you television, sports, salad bars and treat your family nice. They coddle you while they bury you for a hundred years. Rather than lock you in a cell and throw away the key, they put you in a cell and throw the cell away. Believe me, I'm not putting up a sucker's holler. But let's put the truth on the table. What I got is a slow death sentence. They'd be doing me a favour if they put me in the electric chair and ended the story once and for all.’

Donald 'Tony the Greek' Frankos:

‘Behind prison walls there is no mercy for the weak and powerless, no respite from the demands of the hood who has nothing but disgust for his victim's weakness. Guys in the joint will sodomize a ninety-year-old man.’

...on establishing one's position:

‘An obese piece-of-shit made drug dealer, part of the famous Pleasant Avenue connection, named fat Gigi Inglese told me one day in the yard to get water for coffee. “You don't tell nobody to bring water,” I snarled. “In here, you fat motherfucking pig, everybody is the same.” I buried my fist up to the wrist in his large, doughy midsection, and he stumbled away gasping for breath.’

Edward Kuznetsov, *Russian airplane hi-jacker, on his experiences in Soviet prisons:*

‘I have seen convicts swallow huge numbers of nails and quantities of barbed wire; swallow mercury thermometers, pewter tureens (after breaking them into edible portions), chess pieces, needles, ground glass, knives and spoons.

I have seen convicts sew up their eyelids with thread and wire; sew rows of buttons to their bodies; nail their scrotum to the bed...

I have seen convicts cut open the skin of their arms or legs and peel it off as if it were a stocking, or cut lumps of flesh from their belly, roast them and eat them; or cut off their fingers or nose or ears or penis – there is absolutely nothing that they will not do.’

Ronnie Knight*'s recollection of Wandsworth Prison:*

‘Not so much another nick as another planet, inhabited by creatures of a different species... on both sides of the bars. They send you there to get a short, sharp shock. And credit where it's due, that is precisely what you get. In that joint anything terrible that has happened before suddenly becomes a trip down memory lane. You look back on the previous bad times with a degree of fondness. In Wandsworth your soul is exposed.❜

John McVicar:

❛I served about two and a half years in Wandsworth Prison. Known to convicts and criminals as the Hate Factory, Wandsworth has no pretensions to civilised life, no facilities and no amenities. Its main function is to fill the con with enough hate to ensure he comes straight back.❜

❛...You die into the future and spend your time regretting the past. The anti-molly-coddlers; what do they know about the difference it makes to be in prison? The fact of being in prison is everything; nothing else means anything.❜

Jeffrey Archer, *jailed politician and novelist, on the food in Belmarsh Prison:*

❛At noon I'm let out of my cell to join the queue for lunch. One look at what is on offer and I can't face it – overcooked meat, heaven knows from which animal, mushy peas swimming in water and potatoes that Oliver twist would have rejected.❜

Denis Nilsen, *on food in Brixton:*

‘It is perfectly feasible to eat normal rations here and still remain effectively on hunger strike.’

‘...The prison shepherd puts a strong guard on the ninety nine in the fold who want to get out. He goes out to seek the lost sheep and when he finds it he cuts its throat because it will not fit into the fold.’

Jim Phelan, *on Dartmoor Prison:*

‘There is no hollow veneer of culture, no empty prattle of prison reform at the Moor. This is a place where the convict gangs are held at forced labour, under the musket and cutlass and club... This place was tough – tough till it hurt. But at least the warders and officials didn't pretend that it was some sort of training school or course in civics.’

...on the unpopular governor, Colonel Hales:

‘He strode around Parkhurst, like Ajax defying the lightning, knowing that the vile, terrible murderers and burglars were quaking as he passed, knowing that they were only restrained from raping servant girls on Parkhurst main road, and from murdering the errand boys on Rockwood Avenue because he, Hales, was there to hold the desperate monsters down.’

...on the value of tobacco in jail:

‘For an inch of snout a convict could get a clean shirt from a laundryman, a beef dinner from a cook, a couple of decent books from the librarian, a pair of shoes from the boot-maker.

For three inches he could hire a bodyguard or he could buy a decent job from a tobacco-less job holder, or purchase love of a kind among the willowy young effeminates who undulated in every working party.’

George Smithson, *burglar of the 1920s, on his feelings at being sent to penal servitude:*

‘It is no use now recapitulating the bitter feelings I underwent or describing the terrible loneliness that took possession of me when it finally came home to me that it would be a long, long time before I again tasted the joys of freedom. There is no sensation in the world comparable to being securely confined in a cold and dreary cell, forbidden to speak to your fellow beings, shut up at night with only your own wretched thoughts to keep you company. Then you know that crime doesn't pay.’

‘...For the benefit of any aspiring youth who is contemplating a life of crime, I can say without hesitation that the first taste of prison is easily the worst.’

Jack Henry Abbot *who murdered for a second time after being released from a U.S. penitentiary:*

‘No one has ever come out of prison a better man.’

Horatio Bottomley, *crooked MP., on release from his seven year prison sentence:*

‘I am in better health and spirits than I have been for twenty years.’

Billy Hill, *on pounding bones as a prison punishment:*

'The stench of the decaying bones was vile. Then I got used to that, because once or twice I was sick and when I did spew I hurt my stomach. I was sick all over myself. I knocked my body against the cubicle. It was uncomfortable when I was sick. So I was not sick any more.'

Roger Casement, *Irish patriot hanged for treason at Pentonville in 1916:*

'Don't let my body lie in this dreadful place. Take me back to Ireland.'

Jonathan Aitken, *former government minister jailed for perjury, on his fellow prisoners:*

'They thought I was a miracle worker. Small queues used to form outside my cell door.'

Jo le Moko, *French gangster, on his release from seven years solitary confinement in Fresnes Prison, Paris:*

'It gave me the chance to read Balzac from beginning to end.'

Edward Bunker, *on years of effort to be published as a writer after years in prison:*

'When you're not locked up, you're locked out.'

Albert Spaggiari:

'Prison? I've had some of the most beautiful daydreams in the filthiest jails...There are some things worse than doing time. Why else would a guy go back to prison once he's cut his initials on the wall?'

Don Vito Cascioferro, *Sicilian Mafiosi, who spent the last twenty years of his life in prison:*

‘Prison, sickness and necessity reveal the real heart of a man.’

Ruby Sparks, *on first impressions:*

‘When we arrived at Dartmoor, this youngster fell down in a dead faint and nearly pulled the wrists off the two convicts fastened to him. I wasn’t surprised that any sensitive soul like him should faint at the sight of Dartmoor. It’s a horrible sight to see, looming at you through the mist. It gave even me a chasm in my stomach, like finding a frog in your teacup. And I’d just done ten years in the place, whereas he’d never been farther afield than the comforts of Wormwood Scrubs.’

Ted Cole, *bank robber and jailbreaker, on arrival at Alcatraz to begin a fifty year sentence:*

‘Don’t think I’ll like it here. Doubt I’ll stay long.’

Lucky Luciano, *recalling first going to prison:*

‘I seen a movie called Oliver Twist. It was written by some English guy by the name of Charles Dickens and the young kid in that picture reminded me of myself because they used to knock this little bastard around in the picture the way they did to me at Hampton Farms.’

Taki Theodoracopulos, *millionaire socialite, sent to Pentonville for cocaine offences:*

‘The first day in prison is like the first day at boarding school.’

Howard Marks, *on why Spanish prisons are better than those in the UK and America:*

‘You’re allowed a fuck once a month, that makes a hell of a difference.’

John Steele, *from Perth Prison, Scotland in 1991:*

‘It is time we opened our eyes. Our prison system is geared to torment its human stock., to lock us away in concrete tombs and cages, degrade us, strip us of our identity, punish us mentally and physically and leave us to rot and die a thousand deaths in the space of years or even months. With its constant misery, pain, deaths, psychiatric hospitals, and of course riots and escapes, the system has failed prisoners and society. Who, I wonder and ask, does it serve a purpose to? And what reason is there to encourage and condone such a system? One doesn’t need to be a philosopher to help solve the problem, but one would certainly have to be unstable to want to keep it as it is.’

Kris Krishnamma, *jailed drug smuggler-turned author:*

‘Imagine if you can, a hospital where the sick are taken in and made worse; where legless men are admitted to have their arms amputated; where cases of cholera are infected with smallpox for good measure; and where men who once believed they were Napoleon come out thinking they are Caesar as well. Imagine, too the crazy panel of doctors, consultants and scientists, who formulate the policies of such a hospital; holding board meetings, attending conferences, issuing directives, pontificating theories; to be passed on to the mindless lower echelons to be implemented.

Could such a gruesome anomaly survive as a credible institution? It does, it thrives, all over the world; and one of the most vigorous and self-aggrandizing of its associates is called the British penal system. A powerful, politically persuasive unit of society, that encourages the growth of crime while purporting to limit it.’

Charlie Richardson,
South London gangleader, on prison officers.

‘Whereas some men would run away to the Foreign Legion to recover from a disastrous love affair, others ran to the Prison Service to forget that they were members of the human race.’

‘...A lot is said by sociologists, criminologists, psychologists, journalists and politicians about the prisons being full of inadequate people who are a danger to society. They are absolutely right. The screws who work in prisons are usually inadequate and if society didn't keep them in jail they could be a real danger to the public.’

Razor Smith, *imprisoned London robber, on his relationship with prison officers:*

‘I still have a tendency to bite the heads off blatantly stupid, wet-behind-the-ears, couldn't-get-a-ride-in-a-brothel with £50-notes-pinned-all-over-them screws.’

Trevor Hercules, *prisoner-turned author, on life in Albany, a maximum security prison:*

‘The bells that were placed around the wings were for the screws to press whenever there was any trouble. but the inmates took to ringing them, "so the screws could earn their pay". It was great fun to watch the screws tearing round the wings like chickens who had lost their heads. While there, I personally saw at least three screws have heart attacks – and all the inmates cheered as they were carried away on stretchers. Hard men, hard games!’

Ruby Sparks, *on prison cuisine:*

‘At Dartmoor I chewed away nearly all my wooden table in the punishment block. Ate it, mouthful by mouthful, swallowing the chewed pulp of splinters to fill out an empty stomach.

The table wasn't anything tasty. It was just a scrubbed wooden ledge, soggy from years of Dartmoor's eternal dampness. Its flavour was soap and firewood. But I'd eaten it. The lot!

The screws had me up for this, of course. Even a prison governor, you might think, would get a peculiar feeling when a man was fetched up in front of him for eating his wooden table because he was that hungry. You'd suppose a prison governor, wiping the dribble of bacon and eggs off his own plump chin, would have hesitated before edicting more bread-and-water as punishment for a starved convict who had scoffed his table.

But not him. More bread-and-water was what I got. So they carpentered a new table into my cell, and I did my best to eat that, too.’

Wilfred Macartney, *jailed as a communist spy in the 1920s, on prison officers:*

‘When the odds are six to one in their favour, they are able and willing to ‘man-handle’ half-starved convicts, but when the shoe is on the other foot they go down on their knees and beg for mercy.’

Christopher Parnell, *on the murder of a prison guard in an Indonesian prison:*

‘When the prisoners who put him in the steamer tried to pull him out the following morning, he virtually dissolved in their hands. The meat was steamed off the bones, like that of an over-cooked chicken. His cooked flesh was a greyish colour, with a spiteful odour about it.’

Denis Malone, *Governor of Dartmoor, to Frank ‘The Mad Axeman’ Mitchell who picked picked him up and held him in the air:*

‘Now Frank, be a good chap and put me down.’

Willie Sutton, *American bank robber:*

‘For some reason people are under a misapprehension that everybody in prison is a stand-up guy. Far from it. You have to know exactly who you’re dealing with – the rat quotient is very high.’

Taki Theodoracopulos,
millionaire socialite convicted of drug charges:

“There are no guilty men among us. Everyone has been “fitted up”. Even the man I was handcuffed to on my way to Pentonville, the nice Ghanaian, said something about it wasn’t his fault he had been caught with a mountain of dope. I guess whining and lying to oneself is part of criminal behaviour, and most criminals are liars and whiners. None of the men I’ve met up to now seem ever to have heard of that old chestnut, “If you can’t do the time, don’t do the crime.””

Nathan Leopold, *of Leopold and Loeb, the Chicago murderers who were jailed for ninety nine years in the 1920s:*

“The good hood minds his own business. He may disapprove very much of what some other con is doing but unless it directly affects him adversely, he merely shrugs and walks away.”

Bob King, *London armed robber who took up education in jail:*

“I remember when I had done about a year of my degree and I had just learnt what the pecking order in society meant, coming into my cell and saying to another bloke “Hey fuck off my bed, I’m higher up in the pecking order than you.” And he goes “Whaaat?” – looking at me as though I was cracking up. And I said “Didn’t you know there was this German bloke who studied the feeding habits of chickens and worked out a theory of how we all fit into society?” My few mates in jail used to think, I’m sure, that I wasn’t all there.”

College Harry, *old-time London villain, on prison cricket:*

❛Owing to the many different types of criminal that the war had brought to Parkhurst, it was decided to pick teams by the type of crime that each member had committed. Thus we had the Old Lags' Eleven, the Screwsmen's Eleven, the Habitual Criminals' Eleven, the Whizz-Mob Eleven and the North of England and South of England Pickpockets' Elevens. Personally I had never been particularly good at cricket, but I was picked for the Old Lag's Eleven because of my speed in the outfield.❜

Harry Roberts, *police killer, who has spent almost thirty years in prison, with no foreseeable release date:*

❛Once I asked a governor why they wouldn't let me out. He said it was because I was institutionalised. They keep me in here all these years – and then they tell me that!❜

Tony Lambrianou, *on the life sentence he served for his activities with the Krays:*

❛I think about how long I did and I try to remember the seventies. I can't.❜

Eddie Guerin, *bank robber, who served time in British and American jails and escaped from the French penal settlement of French Guiana:*

❛When you have been in and out of jail for the best years that God gave you, you realise, when it is far too late, what an infernal fool you have been. There's nothing clever in going to prison; the real clever men keep out of it.❜

Hugh Collins, *on leaving prison after a life sentence:*

"In prison, the authorities always say "It's a normal world out there, how are you going to fit back into society?" I walked out and found total chaos."

Party Pieces

Ronnie Kray, *on being charged with murder:*

❛I presume that your presumptions are precisely incorrect and that your sarcastic insinuations are too obnoxious to be appreciated.❜

...to the congregation at his brother Ronnie's first wedding:

❛Sing, fuck you! Sing!❜

...on the inconvenience of having to be present at his Old Bailey trial for murder:

❛If I wasn't here now I'd probably be drinking with Judy Garland.❜

Dr Edward Pritchard, *19th Century Glasgow murderer, whose curious grasp of geography did not prevent him giving lectures about his world travels:*

❛I have plucked the eaglets from their eyries in the deserts of Arabia and hunted the Nubian lion in the prairies of North America.❜

John Steele, *on being sent to see a psychiatrist while at a Scottish approved school:*

“I had heard much about these doctors – it was rumoured that they decided who was and who was not a “loony”. The atmosphere in the little room was horrible and frightening. One question he asked me was, “If I gave you a billiard ball and a knife, would you peel it for me?” My pals, who had seen other psychiatrists before had warned me about this. The answer to give is, “Yes, I’ll peel it if you’ll eat it!””

James Gridley, *a witness in the 1953 trial of Alfred Hinds, responding to a suggestion that he was inventing evidence:*

“Never on your life sir! May God strike me blind! And I am a blind guide; I have got an auntie who is blind. I would not tell lies like that on my oath or any Bible.”

Detective Sergeant Harold Challenor, *as he brushed the coat lapel of a man he felt ought to go to prison:*

“I thought I saw some porridge on your suit.”

Big Bill Thompson, *anti-prohibitionist Mayor of Chicago:*

“I’m wetter than the middle of the Atlantic Ocean.”

Leo Brothers, *Chicago hitman, sentenced to fourteen years for first degree murder:*

“I can do that standing on my head.”

Dominique Muzziotti, *French gunman, announcing his retirement from crime:*

“I’ve hung my rod up behind the kitchen stove.”

Willie Moretti, *New Jersey gangster, negotiating Frank Sinatra's departure from the Tommy Dorsey Band by sticking a gun in the bandleader's mouth:*

‘I'm gonna make you an offer you can't refuse.’

Al Capone:

‘I've been accused of every death except the casualty list of the Great War.’

...denying that he was extending his operations:

‘Canada? Why, I don't even know what street it's on!’

Abe 'Kid Twist' Reles, *to Rocco Morganti, before responding to the latter's winning poker hand by shooting him dead:*

‘I'll see you and bump you.’

Arnold Rothstein, *after losing $320,000 in a game of poker:*

‘I'll pay off in day or two. I don't carry that kind of dough around under my fingernails.’

Howard Marks, *international drug dealer, to police as they broke down his door in a 2am raid:*

‘I suppose you've come about the TV licence.’

Clyde Barrow, *who claimed to have the same attitude towards gunfighting as Billy the Kid:*

‘It's a game for two – and I get there first.’

Jacques Mesrine, *French bank robber, to a clerk who accidentally set off an alarm bell:*

‘Don't worry, I like to work to music.’

Ethel Le Neve, *Dr Crippen's lover, on her interest in trains:*

‘There are few things that interest me more than an engine.’

Tony Wild, *supergrass, giving evidence at the OldBailey, to Mr Justice Swanwick:*

‘May I sit down, my lord? I have a fissure on my anus.’

Bugs Moran, *to reporters, having been questioned by the police:*

‘Gentlemen, my wife. If anyone comes calling for me you can tell them this is our wedding anniversary and we're going roller skating.’

Sonny Capone, *son of Al, on being arrested for shoplifting:*

‘Everybody has a little larceny in him I guess.’

Charles Macarthur, *journalist, to his colleague Ben Hecht, as murderer Carl Wanderer stood on the gallows and, instead of reading a speech they had written for him, sang the ballad "Dear Old Pal of Mine":*

‘You know Ben, that son-of-a-bitch should have been a song plugger.’

Duane 'Dog' Chapman, *bounty hunter, who claims to have tracked down 6,000 wanted men and women:*

‘Born on a mountain top, raised in cave, arresting fugitives is all I crave.’

Frank Capone, *who settled matters with bullets rather than words:*

‘You never get no back talk from no corpse.’

John Gotti, *caught on secret police tapes:*

‘This grim reaper, where is he, this fuckin' bum?’

Charlie Richardson, *London gangleader who took a sociology course in prison :*

‘In terms of the sub-culture in which I was socialised in South London streets, it was the norm that disputes between man and man be settled between man and man. Referral to outside agencies such as the police or courts would have been defined as deviant and have led to social ostracism and even worse. This perspective was a central and integral part of my value spectrum.’

Charlie Kray:

‘They say all coppers are bastards. They're not all - but those that are make a very good job of it.’

Teddy Martin, *Glasgow villain, to a bystander as he lay on the ground, bleeding from serious gunshot wounds.*

‘Look in the top pocket of my jacket and see if the bullet broke my reading glasses.’

Jeffrey Archer, *jailed politician and novelist, revealing his sartorial elegance to the warders of Belmarsh Prison:*

‘An officer asks me to stand under and arc light and strip. I take off my jacket, then my tie, followed by my shirt. “Aquascutum, Hilditch and Key and YSL” says the officer, while another writes down this information...I am then asked to slip off my shoes, socks, trousers and pants – “Church's Aquascutum and Calvin Klein.”’

Frank Costello, *Boss of Bosses,who did not like to be reminded of his early days as a cheap hoodlum:*

‘Tough times make monkeys eat red pepper.’

Benjamin ‘Bugsy’ Siegel, *speaking in Los Angeles:*

‘Why don't we move to Vegas? It's the coming country.’

Carmine Galante, *New York mafioso, asked about the risks to his life, shortly before he was murdered:*

‘No one will ever kill me, they wouldn’t dare.’

Joe Yacovelli, *Mafia captain, instructing the hitman who was to kill his rival, Crazy Joe Gallo, in a New York restaurant:*

‘Don’t kill the women. Whack anybody who gets in the way, but don’t touch the girls. That’s disrespectful.’

George ‘Machine Gun’ Kelly, *cornered in Memphis by FBI agents, in an utterance that brought about the latters’ nickname:*

‘Don’t shoot, G-Men, don’t shoot!’

Judge H.C. Leon:

‘I think a judge should be looked upon rather as a sphinx than as a person – you shouldn’t be able to imagine a judge having a bath.’

Peter Sutcliffe, *The Yorkshire Ripper – written on a card, found by police in the cab of his lorry:*

‘In this truck is a man whose latent genius, if unleashed, would rock the nations, whose dynamic energy would overpower those around him. Better let him sleep?’

Charles Manson, *appearing in court with his head shaven:*

‘I am the Devil and the Devil always has a bald head.’

Charles ‘Tex’ Watson, *a Manson follower, to a victim prior to killing him:*

‘I am the Devil and I’m here to do the Devil’s business.’

Donald Hume, *charged in a Swiss court:*

‘I have pleaded guilty to shooting someone. What more do you want? Do you want me to take my teeth out?’

Chopper Read, *Australian hoodlum-turned author, removing his teeth during an interview on Australian television:*

‘These are the James Bond, the carte blanche, the Rolls Royce of false teeth and I’d like you to pay some form of fucking respect to these false teeth.’

Mary Wilson, *who murdered three husbands and a lover, to the caterer at one of her weddings:*

‘Save the left-over cakes. They will come in handy for the funeral.’

Charles Bronson, *after taking two Iraqis and another inmate hostage in Belmarsh Prison:*

‘Sure, I said I’d eat one of the Iraqis, but in my heart of hearts I never really meant it. I’ve got a rule of thumb that says I should never attempt to eat anything that disagrees with me. Plus, I’d had a big breakfast that morning.’

Cynthia Payne, *brothel keeper, asked at her trial if, during her sex parties, she herself went upstairs with any men:*

‘No, I was too busy making sandwiches, seeing they don't drink too much and seeing they don't put cigarette burns on the carpet.’

Graham Young, *the St Albans the St Albans poisoner, informing his sister of his imminent release from Broadmoor, the hospital for the criminally insane where he had been sent after murdering his stepmother:*

‘The pot is now almost boiling. Just think, Win, another few months and your friendly neighbourhood Frankenstein will be at liberty once again.’

Joe Delaney, *New Jersey police chief:*

‘When these organised-crime figures go on trial they all show up in wheelchairs or on crutches. Suddenly they have bad hearts or livers and are about to die. Of course after the case they're all very healthy again. They must go to Lourdes and get cured. Even Butchie Miceli walked away, without his crutches. This guy had multiple sclerosis. Found a cure the minute they said ‘Probation!’ Great cure.’

A neighbour of Ed Gein, *killer, grave robber and role model for Psycho:*

‘Halloween came a little late this year.’

Kate Kray, *on her former husband, Ronnie Kray's dietary concerns:*

‘One day he told me he wasn't going to eat meat any more because of the dangers of mad cow disease. I said “Ron, you're mad already. That's why you're in Broadmoor.”’

Joseph 'Yellow Kid' Weil, *in 1908, asked by a policeman how he came to have $10,000 on him:*

'Oh, that's just walk-about money.'

Abe 'Kid Twist' Reles, *boasting in court of a killing he and a partner in Murder Inc, "Pittsburgh Phil" Strauss, had committed at the behest of Lucky Luciano:*

'It handed Phil a laugh. We left the bum under a billboard that says "Drive Safely". Lucky was satisfied plenty.'

An Irish Garda, *on the pusuit of Martin Cahill – 'The General':*

'Once or twice we'd stop him and he'd pull out a tape recorder and start dictating his protest into it. Then he'd pull down his trousers and show us his Mickey Mouse underpants. Several times we left him without them.'

Nathan Leopold, *to his fellow in teenage murder, Richard Loeb:*

'The Superman is not liable for anything he may do, except for the one crime that it is possible for him to commit - to make a mistake.'

Denis Nilsen, *serial killer, asked by police as to how many bodies lay under the floorboards at any one time:*

'I am not sure. I did not do a stock check.'

Ronnie Biggs, *fugitive Great Train Robber, explaining his reasons for making a record, 'No one Is Innocent' with the outrageous punk group The Sex Pistols:*

'Some have been nauseated by the words, many others have criticised them as not being in good taste, particularly because in one line I say "God save Martin Bormann". But my objective was to show that if we are going to live in and make a better Christian society, then we must start with some basic tenets, and the most fundamental of those is forgiveness for everyone. We cannot discriminate between Martin Bormann and the Good Samaritan.’

Harry Roberts, *police killer, to a psychologist who said his paintings showed his emotional turmoil:*

‘What turmoil? I got the idea from a picture on the cover of Marvel comic.’

Margaret Allen, *a bus conductress, explaining why she had battered to death another woman:*

‘I was in one of my funny moods.’

Donald ‘Pee Wee’ Gaskins, *serial killer, who was the focus of much press attention during the eight years he spent waiting to go to the electric chair:*

‘I don’t think that most of the reporters and other writers I talked to ever gave a rat’s ass about what I truly thought or felt about anything. They just wanted to warm up old turds for the smells, so that was what I served them.’

Taters Chatham, *retired burglar, on his victims and their losses:*

‘They were usually very rich people, millionaires. Some of them regarded it as a nice thing to talk about at dinner parties.’

Peter Scott, *cat-burglar:*

‘The police don’t get terribly excited about people who burgle prefabs in Catford, who haven’t got the ear of the Home Secretary – all my victims were very prestigious people – the only people who end up with vast amounts of money or jewellery are very greedy, predatory people and it's been one of the great privileges of my life to persecute them. I almost feel as though I was an agent of God bringing retribution to the self-satisfied.❜

John Gotti, *known as The Teflon Don until he was convicted and served the rest of his life in Marion Penitentinary:*

❛One thing I ain't gonna be is two-faced. I'm gonna call 'em like I see 'em...I'd like to kill all the lawyers.❜

...revealing hungry feelings on secret police tapes:

❛All I want is a good sandwich. All I want is a good sandwich. You see this sandwich here? This tuna sandwich? That's all I want, a good sandwich.❜

James la Rossa, *New York lawyer who defended many alleged Mafia bosses:*

❛From all of my experience, both as a former Justice Department employee and as a defence attorney, I've never seen evidence that there is a Mafia or any real connection with Italy in any fashion.❜

Taki Theodoracopulos, *millionaire socialite who was imprisoned in Pentonville in 1984 for cocaine offences, on communication difficulties with a warder:*

‘The supervisor is once again complaining about my lack of output, and I tell him that I have no experience with machines. “You’re the worst I’ve ever seen,” he tells me, and I can’t help asking him if Oscar Wilde – who spent two nights in Pentonville – was any better. “If you think I keep records of who comes in here you’re mistaken,” he answers.’

Robert Fabian, *Fabian of the Yard:*

‘Anybody can become a witch. All you have to do is to recite an ancient spell that will conjure up the devil. You then dip a quill pen in blood from your veins and sign an agreement selling him your soul. He gives you a silver coin in token, and leaves you with a cat, a bird and a black dog which will act as your fiendish servant and obey your commands. Such is the ritual of black witchery, and you should be warned that it is an offence under the Witchcraft Act of 1735, which is still unrepealed upon the statute books. When you have become a witch you can put the evil eye on your neighbours, make their cattle die, their crops rot.’

James Maybrick, *Liverpool cotton broker, later poisoned by his wife, speaking to a friend of his penchant for drinking arsenic as a tonic and aphrodisiac:*

‘It is meat and liquor to me. I don't tell everybody. I take it when I can get it but the doctors won't put any into my medicine except now and then. That only tantalises me.’

Pete Gillett, *friend of the Krays:*

‘Crime is very glamorous really. You see, if you want to get a lot of money from property deals you've got to have some money in the first place and the only way to get that is to take it. If you get a job these days for a salary of twenty grand – it costs twenty grand to live, doesn't it? So you're never going to have any spare money for property developments.’

Leonard Hill, *Hong Kong narcotics detective, on methods drug smugglers employ:*

‘We've had cases of a courier who has swallowed a whole lot of male contraceptives tied together in a sausage-like chain, each with about half an ounce of prepared opium or heroin in it. He swallows them all and waits until nature takes its course and then, as soon as one comes out, he pulls the whole lot out one after the other! The largest amount we have ever found was fifty-nine contarceptives, all tied together inside one person.’

Bribery and Corruption

Al Capone, *on corruption in public office:*

‘A crook is a crook, and there’s something healthy about his frankness in the matter. But any guy who pretends that he is enforcing the law and steals on his authority is a swell snake. The worse type of these punks is the big politician.’

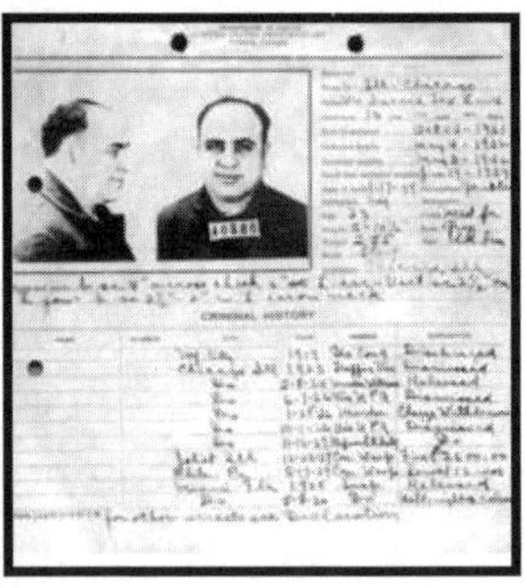

‘They talk about me not being on the legitimate. Nobody’s on the legit. You know that and so do they. Your brother or your father gets in a jam. What do you do? Do you sit back and let him go over the road, without trying to help him? You’d be a yellow dog if you did. Nobody’s on the legit when it comes down to cases.’

Chicago police agent, *days before Al Capone's trial for tax evasion began:*

'The boys are out talking to jurors with a wad of dough in one hand and a gun in the other.'

The warden of Eastern Penitentiary, *to newsmen, after secretly releasing Al Capone from a short sentence:*

'We stuck one in your eye that time. The big guy's gone. We shot him out in a brown automobile.'

Arnold Rothstein, *New York gangland boss, on self-help:*

'You're always against everyone else and they're trying to outsmart you. You mustn't let them and you have to find a way to outsmart them. If a man is willing to be paid off, I'll pay him off. If I don't, someone else will.'

Richard 'Dixie' Davis, *Chicago gangland lawyer:*

'I soon learned that to run an organised mob you've got to have a politician. You have heard about the suspected link between organised crime and politics. Well, I became the missing link.'

Legs Diamond*'s view of the judiciary:*

'For the right price you can buy any judge.'

Mayor William O'Dwyer *of New York City:*

'It doesn't matter whether it is a banker, a businessman or a gangster, his pocketbook is always attractive.'

Frank Costello, *shown a list of judges who were on the Mafia's payroll:*

'I ought to know, I made most of them.'

Sir David McNee, *Metropolitan Police Commissioner:*

'Corruption in a police force is like sin in a society at large. You will never wholly eradicate it for it is embedded in the greed and selfishness of human nature.'

Walter 'Angel Face' Probyn, *on organised crime:*

'The most organised crime, I think, is that which has involved Scotland Yard. All the big crimes are always mixed up in it. The ten per cent racket originated from there.'

Mr Justice Melford Stevenson, *sentencing a corrupt policemen in the 1970s:*

'You poisoned the wells of criminal justice and set about it deliberately. What is equally bad is that you have betrayed your comrades in the Metropolitan Police Force, which enjoys the respect of the civilised world – what remains of it – and not least the grave aspect of what you have done is to provide material for the crooks, cranks and do-gooders who unite to attack the police whenever opportunity occurs.'

Joe Cannon, *London villain:*

'The Old Bill and the villain, both professionals in their different ways, have the measure of each other, and if a situation that looks like ending in bloody murder can be resolved by a touch of bribery and corruption, then all's well that ends well. There's no trial, which saves the taxpayer's money, the overcrowded prisons don't become more overcrowded, the Old Bill cop a few bob and the villain skips off to Spain with the loot. The only lot to lose out are the insurance companies and they can well afford it. The whole set up may be illegal and immoral, but it's practical.'

John Symonds, *corrupt London detective, in a conversation with a villain who was surreptitiously taping him:*

'Don't forget always to let me know straight away if you need anything because I know people every everywhere. Because I'm in a little firm in a firm. Doesn't matter where, anywhere in London I can get on the phone to someone I know I can trust, that talks the same as me...If you're nicked anywhere in London I can get on the blower to someone in my firm who will know someone somewhere who will get something done.'

Ken Drury, *Flying Squad Commander imprisoned for corruption:*

'During my career, I made a point of mixing with criminals. It is essential that you do so. You cannot expect them to give information about crimes if you ostracise them except when you want information from them.'

A Great Train Robber, *who was not caught, on how he avoided capture:*

'The deal was quite straightforward. I had to pay money to the police and I had to give a big lump of it back so they would look as if they were doing well. It was arranged that about £50,000 would be left in a phone box for them to find. And there was some more for them. Funnily enough, they didn't ask for a lot. It was about £2,000. That's all. Then I had to go in and be interviewed and cleared of suspicion. Mind you, when I went in to see the police, I couldn't be sure that they wouldn't go crooked on me.

And in fact, when I got there, one of the policemen wanted to go crooked on the deal, even after he had the money. But there were only two of them involved and he was talked out of it. I walked out free with the guarantee that although they knew that I'd been on the train, they had their money and I wouldn't be fitted up. That was what I needed. ...Corruption? Back in the 50s and 60s it was rampant.❞

Roy Garner, *London gangster-turned-supergrass, before he turned against his partner, Det Supt Tony Lundy:*

❝They thought they had Lundy as a crooked cozzer working with me. Now that couldn't possibly come to fruition 'cos it wasn't true and Lundy would have sued the pants off everybody. Lundy is not crooked. Now I look you in the eye and say that as many times as you need me to say it.❞

Keith Bryson, *a burglar caught in the home of Scotland Yard detective, Tony Lundy:*

❝Lundy is Lundy...you don't compare him with anyone. He's him. He ain't half fitted some people up.❞

Charlie Richardson, *South London gangleader of the 1960s:*

‘It's hard to know what to do with a jury. They have your life in their hands but you have to talk to them through public school interpreters who wear women's clothes and dusty white wigs. I wanted to take them to one side and say, "Look, I'm not such a bad bloke really. So I have smashed a few people in the mouth because they owe me a few quid, but I've given a fortune to charity, I love my mum and I've got five kids. Tell you what...why don't we all run round to the Savoy for a nice chicken dinner and I can put it all straight."’

...on jury nobbling:

‘We was in court and we heard all the names read out and we looked as they come in and you look at the people as the kind of people you can get into. If a man comes in from the East End you find a man who lives in the next road and you ask him what he is like. If they are nice people they go round and fucking see them for you, you understand what I mean. It's alright that way.’

‘...The City is much more crooked than anything I was ever involved in.’

Luciano Liggio, *the Godfather of Corleone, claiming he was persecuted by corrupt policemen:*

‘The state, while fighting against the Mafia and the mafiosi and people of that sort, spends billions tracking down, pursuing Giuliano or Liggio and many sons of innocent mothers. Rivers of money have disappeared into the hands and pockets of policemen. I could mention some examples, but I shall wait until the right time comes.’

So, you can well understand why the police have an interest in the invention of the existence of the Mafia, and when they realise that the phenomenon is in a declining stage, it is then that they invent a new mafiosi, new Liggios etc.’

Big Tim Sullivan, *New York politician, friend of hoodlums and gangsters, offering an explanation for crime:*

‘The thieves we have down here ain't thieves from choice. They are thieves from necessity and necessity don't know any law. They steal because they need a doctor for some dying one or they steal because there ain't any bread in the house for the children.’

Samuel Ashbridge, *corrupt Mayor of Philadelphia, taking oath in 1904:*

‘I have four years to serve. I want no further office when I am out of this one and I shall get out of this one all there is for Samuel H. Ashbridge.’

Charles Becker, *corrupt New York police lieutenant, giving instructions for one of his enemies to be murdered:*

‘All that's necessary is to walk right up to where he is and blaze away at him and leave the rest to me. Nothing will happen to anybody that does it. Walk up to him and shoot him before a policeman if you want to and nothing will happen.’

Charles Whitman, *New York district attorney, on Charles Becker:*

‘I'm going to get Becker if it's the only thing I ever do. New York is supposed to be the greatest city in the world – but as long as Becker and all those like him are allowed to defy and corrupt every law by which human people live, New York will never be anything but a human sewer.’

...**Becker**, *described by a journalist:*

‘Becker was the System. Like Caesar, all things were rendered unto Becker in the underworld. Like Briareus he had a hundred arms...and more power in the Department than the Commissioner.’

Sasakawa Ryoichi *(Japanese right-wing leader who claimed in the 1970s to have eight million followers) on his past associations with gangsters:*

‘Formerly I had many roughnecks around me. I was their leader. So some may call me a rightist. But I am not a rightist. I am a humanitarian.’

Albert Spaggiari, *French bank robber:*

‘I'm used to doing time. I can tell you that jails don't have much effect on human nature. But experience had taught me that the world wasn't so clean outside those walls, either. Sure, Nice looks great when you see it as a tourist, stopping at the Hotel Negresco for as few days and strolling along the Promenade des Anglais, steering a sailing boat over the Bay des Anges.

...But I mean the inside story. I know enough about the Riviera's seamy side to make your hair stand on end. The immorality and vice would supply me with material for several books.’

Dion O'Bannion, *on a bribe demand from Chicago policemen:*

‘Three hundred dollars! To them bums? Why, I can get them knocked off for half that much.’

J. Edgar Hoover, *as head of the FBI, commenting on Mafia Boss Sam Giancana in a letter to Robert Kennedy, US Attorney General:*

‘He made a donation to the campaign of President Kennedy, but was not getting his money's worth.’

Testimonials

Dr Hawley Harvey Crippen, *celebrated wife-murderer, as recalled by his lover's landlady:*

"I think he was one of the nicest men I ever met."

...described by his former employer:

"He was as docile as a kitten. He was quite incapable of murdering his wife."

John McVicar *correcting someone who described him as a murderer:*

"No, actually I was a bank robber, which in the '60s was a perfectly respectable occupation."

Bo Weinberg, *a lieutenant of Dutch Schultz, described by his lawyer, Richard 'Dixie' Davis:*

'Bo had committed more murders than anyone I ever knew, but even when he was drunk there never seemed to be an ounce of malice in him.'

Ian Brady, *Moors Murderer, on the St Albans Poisoner, Graham Young:*

'His first and only ardent love was murder.'

Robert Stroud, *The Birdman of Alcatraz, and a homosexual, as described by a fellow prisoner:*

'He was as attractive as a barracuda.'

Blackie Audett, *on his accomplice* **John Dillinger**:

'I've heard a lot of people say that Dillinger had shifty, beady eyes. I've even read that in the papers. That just plain wasn't true. He was a man completely without fear and he could look you square in the eye for as long as you could stand it.'

Judge J.D.Williams, *writing to the Clemency Board on behalf of John Dillinger, during the future Public Enemy Number One's first prison sentence*:

'I believe if this prisoner is paroled, that he has learned his lesson and that he will go straight in the future and will make a useful and honourable citizen.'

Big Jim Colosimo, *mentor to Al Capone, described by fellow gangster Ike Bloom:*

'There wasn't a piker's hair in Big Jim's head.

Whatever game he played, he shot straight. He wasn't greedy. He brought the society swells and the millionaires into the redlight district. Big Jim never bilked a pal or turned down a good guy and he always kept his mouth shut.❜

Father Malloy, *a Chicago priest, who attended Dion O' Bannion's funeral against his superior's orders and prayed for the murdered gangster:*

❛It was the least I could do. No matter what he became, he was one of ours at the beginning.❜

Dapper Dan Collins, *New York con man who possessed a fatal appeal to women, described by his attorney:*

❛Collins could meet a woman at nine o'clock in the evening and be holding her hand in ten minutes. By nine in the morning, he'd be holding her bankbook.❜

Ronnie Kray, *on his friend Frank 'The Mad Axeman' Mitchell's extraordinary libido:*

❛He was as randy as a stoat. I've never known a guy like it. He would give a bird one and then give her another one with hardly a pause for breath. Women went wild for him. They'd queue up just to be given one by him. He looked like a gypsy, had a body like Charles Atlas and screwed like a rabbit.It was what you might call a winning combination.❜

William Brodie, *whose double life in Edinburgh as a day-time councillor and night-time robber reputedly led Robert Louis Stevenson to write "Dr Jekyll and Mr Hyde", on his counsel, Henry Erskine:*

❛He's the best cock that ever fought.❜

Clyde Barrow, *in a letter to Henry Ford:*

‘Dear Sir, While I still have got breath in my lungs I will tell you what a dandy car you make. I have drove Fords exclusively when I could get away with one. For sustained speed and freedom from trouble the Ford has got every other car skinned and even if my business hasn't been strictly legal it don't hurt anything to tell you what a fine car you got in the V8. Yours truly, Clyde Champion Barrow.’

Denis Nilsen *the Muswell Hill Killer, to a journalist interviewing him in Albany Prison for a documentary film about serial killers:*

‘With no disrespect, I much prefer Dr Anthony Clair. I'm sure you know your job but I'm a fan of his. I listen to him on Radio 4, he's got a good way about him.’

Al Capone, *on the lawyers who had failed to win him an appeal against his eleven year sentence for tax evasion:*

‘They're overpaid dumb bastards who couldn't spring a pickpocket.’

Bugs Moran *on his great rival:*

‘Capone is low life and he's got a disease he can't get rid of. Everybody knows it.’

Blackie Audett, *on Public Enemy Number One and Alcatraz inmate, Alvin Karpis:*

‘Creepy Karpis was one of the most over-rated bad men that ever drawed a gun. A lot like Al Capone in some ways....Old Creepy come to the rock with a lot of national publicity hanging all over him, like decorations on a Christmas tree. He was a big shot and he didn't want no one to forget it. All he ever wanted was his name in the paper. Whenever he seen that he puffed himself right up, just like a peacock. ...He never done me no great harm, but anybody can have all the stock I might ever own in Alvin Karpis for just packing it away. I wouldn't trust Old Creepy as far as a kid could throw him.❞

Serge Rubinstein, *Russian-born swindler, noticed by the chairman of a British bank as he tried to ingratiate himself in London society:*

❝Who is that little runt?
He reminds me of a lovesick bull!❞

Robert Merkle, *attorney, on Carlos Lehder:*

❝He was to cocaine transportation as Henry Ford was to automobiles.❞

James Nash, *London villain on remand for murder, as recalled by Scotland Yard's* **Bert Wickstead**:

❝He had a very quiet voice for such a violent man, but I don't recall him saying anything that seemed worth remembering. He was a man of negative values – a non-smoker, non-drinker, who ate a pound of boiled sweets every day. He would sit in his cell, chewing them endlessly. Judging by the expression on his face he could have been on another planet.❞

Edward Bunker, *convict turned author and film actor, on American justice:*

❝We say our system is the best – by what criteria? Do we free the innocent and punish the guilty better than others? We do alright unless the guilty are rich, but nobody manages to punish the rich very much.❞

Arthur Harding, *London villain of the early 1900s, on a contemporary in the East End underworld:*

‘The man they called Scabby...would pick his victims from people who showed fear and make them give him money for protection. One night in a doss-house in Dorset Street Scabby came in with a parcel of fish and chips. He offered the chips round, which was the custom then and still is. But one drunken fool took his piece of fish instead of just the chips and started eating it. Scabby had a knife in his hand, because he was about to cut a loaf of bread. When he realised what had happened he stabbed the man fatally. He was put on trial for murder, pleaded provocation and was acquitted. Later, after drinking in the Frying Pan, a pub at the corner of Thrawl Street and Brick Lane, he crossed the road, walked into Mother Wolff's, picked up a penny cake and walked out of the shop without paying, after using some threats. He was charged with stealing a penny cake and sentenced to 12 months jail. Such is justice.’

Charlie Peace, *Victorian murderer and womaniser, described by his former mistress:*

‘Not even Shakespeare could adequately paint such a man as he has been My life-long regret will be that I ever knew him.’

Police officer *to Glasgow villain Thomas Campbell, after his arrest for the Glasgow Ice- Cream murders:*

‘You have spent your life creating the reputation of being a violent monster. Now that monster is going to turn around and bite you.’

Dayton Leroy Rogers, *US killer of seven prostitutes, as described by his prosecutor to a jury:*

‘That person is a walking time bomb. That person is an act of criminal violence looking for a place to happen. He’s capable of fooling psychologists. He’s capable of fooling psychiatrists. I hope to God he’s not capable of fooling you.’

California police officer, *after describing* **Robert Ramirez**, *the Night Stalker – before his identity was known, as ‘a tall thin youth with rotting teeth and curly hair’:*

‘The biggest thing this creep has going against him is that he is so frigging ugly someone is sure to spot him.’

Kodama Yoshio, *Japanese gangster:*

‘There are too many petty hoodlums. It makes me angry to see them loitering around and causing trouble to the passers-by.’

Sammy Lewis, *drug dealer, born in England of West Indian parents:*

‘They are the most disorganised people in the world, the Jamaicans. And most of these so-called Yardies are thick. They blow folks away for the sake of it. That’s what makes them dangerous - very dangerous.’

Elmyr de Hory, *master faker, speaking of the art experts whom he had often deceived:*

‘They know more about fine words than fine art.’

General manager of Broadmoor, *speaking of* **The Yorkshire Ripper** *in 1992:*

‘Peter Sutcliffe is mad, not bad. He is the least of my worries.’

Jim Phelan, *gunman-turned-writer, on the elitism of armed robbers in his day:*

‘They are extravagant, addicted to boasting, often impatient of conventional morality. When they have pulled off a big job they celebrate expensively, laugh defiance of danger past, scorn hypothetical dangers to come. They tend to herd together with their own kind and despise mugs.’

Joe Cannon, *London villain:*

‘What is a villain? By definition he is a violent, malevolent or unscrupulous evil-doer who is low-born and base. What the dictionary does not say is that he lives in a separate world, apart from normal society, a world that lives by its own rules and very rigid codes. It is something the outsider can never hope to understand completely.’

Dave Courtney, *London TV-villain-turned-author:*

‘Villains are like builders but they've got more front and show less arse.’

F.Lee Bailey, *controversial American lawyer:*

‘Most good criminal lawyers are loners. A hundred years ago you saw them walking down some dusty street with a couple of guns, shooting people. That's all gone. Now it's more refined.’

Billie Frechette, *on her former lover,* **John Dillinger**:

‘He likes to dance and he liked to hunt. I think he liked gravy better than anything else. He liked bread and gravy.’

Cornelia Biddle, *Philadelphia socialite, visiting the gunned-down* **Legs Diamond** *in a New York hospital:*

‘He is such a nice little fellow. He's so sweet and such an intelligent sort of person.’

Arnold Rothstein, *described by his attorney:*

‘Rothstein is a man who dwells in doorways...a grey rat, waiting for his cheese. He is preoccupied. He walks woodenly. When he walks the street, he is like a horse in that he can see both sidesas well as ahead. He always walks the kerb line.’

The Boston Strangler*'s employer, in a letter to the police:*

‘Albert was truly a remarkable man...He was completely lovable to every individual while working for me. Never was there any deviation from the highest proper sense of things.’

Mad Frankie Fraser:

‘Billy Benstead was a fantastic man; he came from an impeccable criminal background. He suffered from asthma and even climbing up drainpipes he used the inhaler. He had very long arms and could go up a drainpipe in seconds. But he had a weakness; he was a fantastic gambler, so he had to keep climbing round Belgravia and all the country houses.’

Johnny Ramensky, *Scottish safecracker and folk-hero, described by his solicitor during his last court appearance:*

‘He has been on more roofs than the legendary fiddler.’

Willy Sutton, *the bank robber, recalling old mobster, Dinny Meehan:*

‘He was the only dock boss I can remember who died in bed. By that I mean that somebody slipped in through his bedroom window while he was asleep and put a bullet in his brain.’

Meyer Lansky, *Godfather of Godfathers:*

‘One quarter of us is good. Three quarters is bad. That's a tough fight, three against one.’

Mrs Meyer Lansky, *speaking of her husband, who left a criminal fortune estimated at $400 million:*

‘There was something in this man that was imperial. He reminded me of somebody, like, out of the Bible.’

John McVicar *on London villain, actor and friend-of-the-famous,* **John Bindon:**

‘One of Bindon's many party tricks was to ask for a pint, then flop his 13" member on to the bar and say, "Half a pint for my friend as well." In the Chelsea Arts Club during the 70s this became known as the "Bindon problem" as young *terrably-terrably* Henriettas, who traditionally moonlight there as barmaids, were regularly stretchered out in a state of shock.’

That's A Bit Rich !

Lee Harvey Oswald, *in November 1963:*

'American people will soon forget the President was shot, but I didn't shoot him.'

Ian Brady, *Moors Murderer:*

'There are no saints in this world, only liars, lunatics and journalists.'

Timothy McVeigh, *who planted the Oklahoma City bomb that killed 168 and wounded 600 people:*

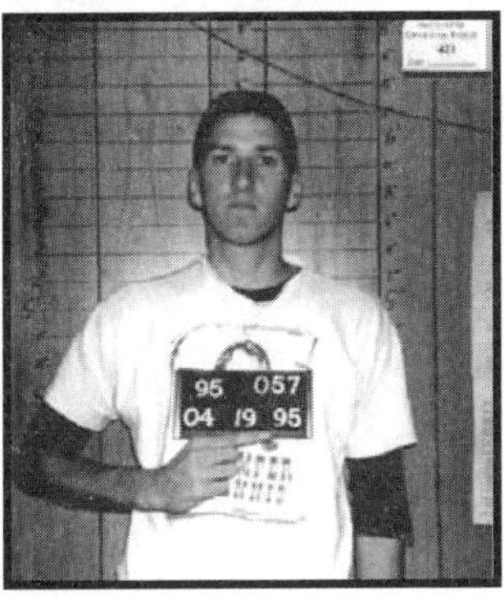

'Like everybody else, I thought it was a tragic event and that's all I really want to say.'

Curtis Warren, *Liverpool drug baron who went international:*

'Everyone's entitled to one bad habit.'

Jonathan Aitken, *former Tory minister, announcing the libel action that would later lead to his imprisonment for perjury:*

❛If it falls to me to start a fight to cut out the cancer of bent and twisted journalism in our country with the simple sword of truth and the trusty shield of fair play, so be it.❜

...to the editor of The Guardian:

❛Are we all bare-faced liars?❜

Christopher Parnell, *sentenced to life imprisonment and a $50,000 fine for drug trafficking in Indonesia:*

❛I was led out to the waiting van and driven back to Krobokan Prison with the judge's orders still ringing in my ears – "You will not die before you pay your fine and you will be kept until you die in prison."❜

Dave Courtney, *London TV-villain-turned author, on organising the security for Ronnie Kray's funeral:*

❛Losing someone like Ron is like losing the monarch. For me he has been lying in state and his funeral is like Sir Winston Churchill's.❜

Albert Donoghue, *Kray henchman who turned Queen's Evidence against them:*

❛The underworld is a different world with its own codes, and you work within those codes.❜

Mad Frankie Fraser, *on 9 November 1980:*

❛This was a bad day for the family. Poor Shirley, Eva's daughter, got nicked for murder. The coppers came round one Sunday and there was the man's head on a plate in her fridge. Just like John the Baptist.❜

Freddie Foreman, *on Blantyre House, an open prison:*

‘Prisoners were expected to engage in some very odd practices. The governor encouraged grown men to do the Hokey Cokey holding hands with screws. I mean to say!’

William F. Howe, *New York defender, after shooting at burglars who broke into his house:*

‘I don't object to burglars as clients – they're pretty good clients – but I seriously object to their operating on my house.’

John Wheater, *solicitor, to police about to search his premises after the Great Train Robbery:*

‘Don't think I'm being rude, but I would like to search you people first.’

Jonathan King, *jailed music mogul on the media's hostility to himself and fellow prisoner Jeffrey Archer:*

‘It's almost as though the great British public have suppurating boils all over themselves and have to keep lancing them to let the bile out.’

Reggie Kray, *in prison:*

‘I have kept my religious views a secret until now...I will be a vehicle of God.’

Henri Landru, *on trial for murder, asked by the judge if he were not an habitual liar:*

‘I am not a lawyer, monsieur.’

Lady Lucan, *wife of the missing Lord, wanted for murder:*

‘My husband was a nobleman.’

Detective Inspector Mike Williams,
on Harold Shipman's arrogance when being questioned:

❛I think he would have liked the Chief Constable to interview him.❜

Al Capone:

❛People respect nothing nowadays. Once we put virtue, honour, truth and the law on a pedestal. Our children were brought up to respect things. But now, look what a mess we've made of life.❜

Rokusuke Tanaka, *Japanese cabinet secretary, asked why a Yakuza gangster was running one of his campaign groups:*

❛It is the responsibility of a politician to rehabilitate ex-convicts.❜

Peter Sutcliffe, *The Yorkshire Ripper, who murdered 13 women and attempted to kill seven more:*

❛There is lot wrong with society today. It's depraved. All they think is money and finances. There are no moral values.❜

❛...It's really awful for anyone to be in pain. I wouldn't be responsible for anyone's agony, ever. Those people I attacked, well it wasn't really me, I mean the real, caring me. That was me in conflict – a good Catholic fighting an avenging angel acting on orders from God. I'm no mass killer. I'd been told what my mission was, like a soldier in a war. I couldn't disobey my orders. They came from the highest authority.❜

Alfredo Messina, *notorious London pimp, to detectives who arrested him for living off immoral earnings:*

‘Let's be friends. We are men of the world and can't afford to fall out. I am going to give you a lovely lunch, with turkey and champagne.’

Rolland McMaster, *a suspect in the killing of Teamsters Union leader, Jimmy Hoffa, whom he said had run off to Brazil with a black go-go dancer:*

‘Teamsters have professional ethics just like reporters. We don't shoot people and kill people. I hired a soothsayer and asked her where Jimmy was. That's what she told me.’

Henry Lee Lucas, *on Death Row in Texas, after confessing to 360 murders:*

‘I'd like the opportunity to tell the truth. I've lived a decent life.’

David Barnard, *convict who escaped from Wormwood Scrubs and returned his prison clothes, in a note to the Governor:*

‘Dear Guv, I don't want you to think I'm so low as to steal your clothes, so I am returning them except for the shoes as it hurts to walk barefoot in London. Love...’

Bella Gunness, *American turn-of-the-century mass murderer, explaining how a hatchet came to be buried in the head of her deceased husband:*

‘It slipped from a shelf.’

John Wayne Gacy, *claiming he should not have been convicted because the search warrant on his house was invalid:*

‘It's the theory of fruit from a poisoned tree. The first warrant is poisoned. All the fruit they got from that is poisoned.’

Alrich Ames, *highest ranking CIA agent ever to spy for the Soviet Union:*

‘Frankly, these spy wars are a sideshow which have had no real impact on our security interests over the years.’

Harold Shipman, *asked in late February how long a sick patient was likely to live:*

‘I wouldn't buy him an Easter egg.’

Clarence Darrow, *the great American defence lawyer, described by a colleague's wife:*

‘He was one of the dirtiest men I ever saw. His nails were dirty, his ears were dirty.’

Kenneth Noye, *who stabbed a man to death in a road-rage argument, explaining why he carried a knife:*

‘I would have preferred a stun gun or CS gas but they are illegal.’

Taruvingia Howe, *a Zimbabwean, asked by a magistrate why he stole 757 sweaters, 733 men's shirts, 460 dresses, 403 jackets, 83 pairs of socks and 286 pairs of children's trousers, worth a round £14,000:*

‘I have a large family.’

Kooks and Crazies

Andrei Chikatilo, *the Russian Ripper, inexplicably dropping his trousers during his trial:*

‘I am not a homosexual. I have milk in my breasts, I am going to give birth.’

Arthur Shawcross, *serial killer, on his perverse sexual habits:*

‘One day I did it to a chicken. It died. Then a cow, dog and a horse.’

Charles Gervais, *murderer:*

‘I’m worse than Charles Manson. I done what I did but I put my own hands in the blood. I hate everything. I always did. I’ve spit in people’s faces. I’ve shook my dick at ’em.’

Christa Lehmann, *German woman who poisoned her husband, her in-laws and a friend:*

‘I don’t suppose I should have done it but I love to go to funerals.’

Brenda Spencer, *seventeen year-old, asked by police in San Diego why she had fired a semi-automatic rifle into a crowded school playground, killing two people and wounding others:*

‘I just did it for the fun of it. I don’t like Mondays. I did it because it’s a way to cheer the day up. Nobody likes Mondays.’

Charlie Starkweather's *note, stuck on the door of his girlfriend's home after he had murdered her family and didn't want to be disturbed from watching television:*

'Stay a Way. Every Body is Sick With the Flu.'

David Koresh, *the Waco cult leader, inviting followers to his wedding:*

'I have seven eyes and seven horns. My name is the Word of God and I ride on a white horse. I am here on earth to give you the Seventh Angel's Message.'

Theodore Kaczynski, *the Unabomber, to his journal:*

'I intend to start killing people. If I am successful at this it is possible that, when I am caught (not alive, I fervently hope!) there will be some speculation in the news media as to my motives. If such speculation occurs, they are bound to make me out to be a sickie. In this connection, I would point out that many times conformist types seem to have a powerful need to depict the enemy of society as sordid, repulsive or sick.'

David Copeland, *the Soho pub bomber:*

'If no one remembers who you are, you never existed.'

'...I have been put on this planet to prove myself, to show myself worthy to rule. I have passed that test.'

Henri Blot, *necrophiliac, to a judge who rebuked him:*

'How would you have it? Every man to his own tastes. Mine is for corpses.'

David Berkowitz, *'Son of Sam', goading police who hunted him:*

'Sam's a thirsty lad and he won't let me stop killing until he gets his fill of blood.'

...after his arrest, asked why he killed people:

'It was a command. I had a sign and I followed it. Sam told me what to do and I did it. His commands came to me through his dog. Sam is the devil.'

Ed Kemper – *serial killer who buried the decapitated heads of his female victims in the back garden – to his mother as she looked out of the window:*

'You know, people really look up to you Mom.'

Ronald True, *on remand in Brixton for the murder of a prostitute, greeting the arrival of Henry Jacoby, a youth later hanged for the murder of Lady White:*

'Here's another for the murderer's club. Only those who kill outright accepted.'

Graham Young, *the St Albans poisoner, in a Christmas card to his dog, after being released from Broadmoor:*

'To whom it may concern: This is to certify that Rupert Beagle has undergone psychoanalysis and, contrary to appearances, is not suffering from hydrophobia or any other canine psychosis. Signed, Sigmund Freud.'

...told after his arrest that one of his victims' condition was deteriorating:

'That concerns me, as it's obvious the doctors are not treating him properly.'

George Hennard, *as he opened fire in a crowded Bell County, Texas restaurant, shooting dead twenty-two people:*

'Time to pay.'

James Shackleton, *funeral director charged with trying to obtain a job in Wormwood Scrubs by deception:*

‘I am fascinated by death. It is in my blood. I get a real kick from being an undertaker and dealing with dead bodies. It makes you feel special.’

Albert De Salvo, *The Boston Strangler recalling sitting at home watching a television newsflash of one of his murders:*

‘I knew it was me who did it, but why I did it and everything else I don't know....I wasn't excited, I didn't think about it. I sat down to dinner and I didn't think about it at all.’

Peter Kurton, *The Monster of Dusseldorf, describing sitting in cafe, close to the scene, the day after one his murders:*

‘I sat there and drank a glass of beer and read all about the murder in the papers. People were talking about it all around me. All this amount of horror and indignation did me good.’

Jack the Ripper, *in a letter, sent to the Central News Agency in London:*

‘I am down on whores and I shant quit ripping them until I do get bucked. Grand work the last job was. I gave the lady no time to squeal.....I love my work and want to start again. You will soon hear of me with my funny little games......The next job I shall clip the lady's ears off and send to the police officers just for jolly wouldnt you....My knife is nice and sharp I want to get to work right away if I get a chance.’

. . . in a letter to police surgeon, Dr Frederick Openshaw, who had examined a kidney taken from the body of a victim:

‘Old boss you was rite it was the left kidney i was

going to hoperate again close to your ospitle just as i was going to dror mi nife along of er bloomin throte them cusses of coppers spoilt the game but i guess i wil be on the job soon and will send you another bit of innerds.......O have you seen the devle with his mikerscope and scalpul a-lookin at a kidney with a slide cocked up.'

John Christie, *murderer of eight women at 10 Rillington Place:*

'Having a cup of tea seems as much a part of my murder career as whisky is with other murderers.'

'...The Sixth Commandment – Thou Shalt Not Kill – fascinated me. I always knew that someday I should defy it.'

'...My first murder was thrilling because I had embarked on the career I had chosen for myself, the career of murder.'

Edward Leonski, *The Singing Strangler, who strangled three women on the streets of Melbourne, explaining that he liked women with soft voices:*

'That's why I choked these ladies – it was to get their voices.'

Patrick Mahon, *who dismembered his lover and placed her in a trunk in the spare bedroom:*

'The damn place was haunted. I wanted some human companionship.'

James Walkden, *Lancashire man found lying drunk in the street, clutching a human skull in a bag:*

'I stole it from the cemetery to put on top of my TV for decoration.'

Frank Vitkovic, *law student, who would later shoot eight people dead and maim five others in an Australian bank:*

‘The world is full of vicious, cruel people.’

answering a question in a property contract law examination:

‘The present criminal laws are a farce. One person has lost all his civil rights (ie has been murdered) while the son of a bitch who killed him is entitled, according to the “civil libertarian philosophy” to have his future considered, his reform considered, his constitutional rights considered, his state of mind considered, the stress he was under, the “so-called” provocation of the deceased (which by the way never occurred but is invented by the defen-dant and taken for granted by idiotic judges), the fact that he only meant to scare the deceased, the gun just “went off”...Warning – prophetic – St Paul.’

Rudolf Pleil, *post-war German serial killer who described himself as ‘der Beste Totmacher’ – the best death maker:*

‘Every man has his passion. Some like whist, I prefer killing people.’

Hans Graewe, *sadistic killer for the Cleveland Mafia, who liked to be known as ‘The Surgeon’ because of his skill in cutting up bodies:*

‘They can’t get me for murder. All I did was commit malpractice.’

Martha Wise, *known in her day as The American Borgia, who poisoned her entire family and, according to her boyfriend, barked like a dog while making love:*

‘It was the devil who told me to do it. He came to me when I was in the kitchen baking bread. He came to me while I was working in the fields. He followed me everywhere.’

Oliver Curtis Perry, *US train robber, described by a Pinkertons detective as "the nerviest outlaw I ever heard of", after devising a machine to blind himself in prison:*

❛I was born in the light of day, against my will, of course. I now assert my right to shut out that light.❜

Mark David Chapman, *killer of John Lennon:*

❛I made a decision to be crazy, or schizophrenic, a psychopath or a sociopath - whatever it is you have to be to do the things that I did. It's a choice anybody can make.❜

❛...Normal kids don't grow up to shoot ex-Beatles....I became the *Catcher in the Rye* of my generation. I became almost a prophet.❜

...on the 'little people' inside his head who had told him to murder John Lennon:

❛They were shocked. They were still part of my conscience and when I didn't follow my conscience there was no longer any government inside of me. I was on my own. Alone in my apartment I would strip naked and put on Beatles records and pray to Satan. I prayed for the demons to enter my body to give me the power to kill. I would scream and screech into a tape recorder "John Lennon must die! John Lennon is a phoney!"❜

Sean Sellars, *sixteen year old Oklahoma Satanist, who murdered his mother, father and a shop assistant:*

❛Dungeons and Dragons got me started. I wanted to learn more about it, so I went to the library and stole some books about dragons, witches, wizards and Satanism.❜

John Wayne Gacy, *speaking to police about the young men he employed in his construction business, many of whom were among his thirty three victims:*

❛I wanted to give young people a chance. Young people always get a raw deal, but if you give them responsibility they rise to the occasion.❜

Robert Chase, *The Dracula Killer, asked why he had murdered his victims:*

❛I had to do it. I have blood poisoning and I need blood. I was tired of hunting and killing animals so I could drink their blood. I thought about it for several weeks and decided I would kill humans for their blood.❜

The Zodiac Killer *who preyed on late 1960s California, and remains undetected to this day, in a letter to a newspaper:*

❛I like to kill people because it is so much fun. To kill someone gives me the most thrilling experience. It is even better than sex. The best part will be when I die. I will be reborn in Paradise and then all I have killed will become my slaves. I will not give you my name because you will try to slow or stop my collecting of slaves for my afterlife.❜

...in another letter:

❛This is the Zodiac speaking. I have become very upset with the people of San Fran Bay area. They have not complied with my wishes for them to wear some nice buttons. I promised to punish them if they did not comply, by animating a full School Bus. But now school is out for the summer, so I punished them in another way. I shot a man sitting in a parked car with a .38.❜

Peter Sutcliffe, *the Yorkshire Ripper, asked by his brother why he had killed thirteen women.*

“I were just cleaning up streets, our kid. Just cleaning up the streets.”

“...Killing prostitutes had become an obsession with me. I could not stop myself. It was like a drug.”

...on his refusal to take medication in Broadmoor:

“If I took drugs the doctors gave me and the voices stopped, that could be dangerous for me. I’d have to admit I was mentally ill and I couldn’t live with that.”

Ian Brady, *Moors Murderer, on Sutcliffe, whom he met in Broadmoor:*

“I had the opportunity to interview Sutcliffe at length when I was passing through the south of England. He had a mild and pleasant mien, his tone of voice quiet and deferential throughout....He spoke of the murders he committed in a matter-of-fact, humdrum manner, sometimes quite humorously.”

Denis Nilsen, *the Muswell Hill killer:*

“The victim is the dirty platter after the feast and the washing up is a clinically ordinary task...Occasionally I hear a piece of music which was playing at the time of my killings – then I become extremely disturbed.”

“If I’d been arrested at sixty-five years of age there might have been thousands of bodies behind me.”

John Haigh, *the Acid Bath Murderer, telling police how he had disposed of his victim:*

‘I shot her in the back of the head while she was examining some paper for use as finger nails. Then I went out to the car and fetched in a drinking glass and made an incision, I think with a penknife, in the side of the throat. I collected a glass of blood, which I then drank. Following that, I removed the coat she was wearing, a Persian lamb, and the jewellery, rings, necklace earrings and cruciform, and put her in a forty-five gallon tank. Before I put the handbag in the tank I took from it the cash – about thirty shillings – and her fountain pen, and kept these, and tipped the rest into the tank with the bag. I then filled the tank up with sulphuric acid...I should have said that in between having her in the tank and pumping in the acid I went round to the Ancient Prior's for a cup of tea.’

Henri Girard, *French murderer who insured his victims before poisoning them:*

‘I have always been unhappy, no one has ever tried to understand me. I will always be misunderstood – abnormal as I have been called – and for all that I am good with a very warm heart.’

Heinrich Pommerencke, *The Beast of the Black Forest who killed twelve victims, attempted to kill a similar amount, raped twenty one times and committed dozens of robberies and other crimes:*

‘When I was a boy I never had a friend in the world.’

Charles Manson:

‘You people who are filled with the fear that I might someday be released: breathe easy, I don’t see it happening. And for you people who are victims of all the hype that portrays me as a charismatic cult leader, guru, lover, Pied Piper or another Jesus, I want you to know I’ve got everything in the world, and beyond, right here. My eyes are cameras. My mind is tuned to more television stations than exist in your world. And it suffers no censorship. Through it, I have a world and the universe as my own. So, save your sympathy and know that only a body is in prison. At my will I walk your streets and am right out there among you.’

...explaining why he appeared in court with an X carved into his forehead:

‘I have X’d myself from your world... You have created the monster...I am not of you, from you, nor do I condone your unjust attitude towards things, animals, and people that you do not try to understand... I stand opposed to what you do and have done in the past...You make fun of the world and have murdered the world in the name of Jesus Christ...My faith in me is stronger than all of your armies, governments, gas chambers, or anything you may want to do to me. I know what I have done. Your courtroom is man’s game. Love is my judge.’

An FBI spokesman:

‘The chosen occupation of today's serial killer is that of a truck driver. These are highly transient killers who travel all over the United States.’

Ted Bundy, *serial killer:*

‘Sometimes I feel like a vampire.’

...to a FBI agent:

‘You're like a fisherman who fishes for years and catches a small fish. Sometimes a medium fish. You get lucky and get a big fish. But you know that there's a really big fish under there that always gets away. You and your group are going to get a lot of serial killers and they're going to help you. But with the real good ones, the only way you are going to know what goes on under the water is to go under the water. The fisherman drowns going underwater. But I can take you there without you drowning. If I trust you. And if I decide.’

A serial-killer groupie *who wrote to* **Ted Bundy** *on Death Row:*

‘I used to date a man in Aspen who told me in gory detail about killing girls, and you're not a bit like him. I can tell from you're nice face that you're a “good guy”. Woman's intuition.’

Richard Speck, *who raped and murdered eight nurses in one night, on hearing of eighteen year old Robert Smith's tally of seven victims, a few months later:*

‘Boy, I'd like to get my hands on that guy, I'd kill him.’

Richard Ramirez, *'The Night Stalker – killer of thirteen people:*

'I don't need to hear all of society's rationalisations. I've heard them all before and the fact remains that what is, is. You don't understand me.You are not expected to. You are not capable of it. I am beyond your experience. I am beyond good and evil... I will be avenged. Lucifer dwells within us all.'

Tahweh Ben Yahweh,
leader of the Yahwehs, a black American sect:

'Kill me a white devil and bring me an ear.'

Jim Jones, *as more than 900 members of his People's Temple died from cyanide poisoning in a mass suicide:*

'They are not crying out of pain. It's just a little bitter tasting.'

Arthur Shawcross, *released killer who went on to murder eleven New York prostitutes:*

'There is too much torment bottled up inside of me,too much anger that needs to be rid of! I should be castrated or have an electrode placed in my head to stop my stupidness or whatever. I'm just a lost soul looking for release of my madness.'

...trying to explain why he murdered them:

'I had a problem. A problem that I couldn't keep an erection, couldn't have an orgasm. My wife knew about it. I went out with at least eighty five to a hundred or more women. I was trying to find out why I was impotent, something like that.'

Lawyer for Arne Johnson, *who claimed he had been forced by demons to murder his next door neighbour:*

‘The courts have dealt with the existence of God before. Now they are going to have to deal with the existence of the Devil.’

Abbe Boudes, *who murdered a fellow priest in France, speaking to a warder:*

‘They think I am mad because I have committed some trifling breaches of the sixth commandment.’

Francis Bloeth, *who shot three people dead in a killing spree on Long Island:*

‘I would have killed more but I was out of ammunition and I was afraid to buy more.’

Howard Unruh, *who killed thirteen inhabitants of Camden, New Jersey in twelve minutes in September 1949:*

‘I’d have killed a thousand if I’d had the ammunition.’

James Huberty, *who shot dead twenty-one customers in a McDonalds restaurant in California, recalled by a neighbour:*

‘He was always a shooting guy...he’d shoot five heads of cabbage and pick one.’

Jeffrey Dahmer, *The Milwaukee Cannibal, on his victims:*

‘My consuming lust was to experience their bodies.’

Jack Tratsart, *sent to Broadmoor for the murder of his father and sister:*

‘This is a world of youth. All men over forty scram.’

Donald 'Pee Wee' Gaskins, *whose victims totalled more than a hundred, looking back on his murderous life, before going to the electric chair in 1991:*

'I was born special and fortunate. I am special and fortunate. I am one of the few that truly understands what death and pain are all about. I have a special kind of mind that allows me to give myself permission to kill.'

'Not many men is privileged to live a life as free and pleasured as mine has been. Once you decide to kill – and I don't mean killing some piss-ant in a bar or two old farts in a hold-up, I'm talking about deciding to kill anybody you want, anytime you want, any where you want, any way you want – once you get to that point, you set yourself free to live the best kind of life there is.'

Verbal Jousts

Frank Costello, *asked by counsel for the Kefauver Investigation into Organised Crime if he had been paid sixty thousand dollarsby a racetrack for doing nothing:*

‘That's right, I did.’
Counsel: ‘Isn't that kind of synonymous with taking candy from a child?’
Costello: ‘No. I know a lot of lawyers that get a fifty thousand dollar fee that's worth only fifteen hundred dollars.’
Counsel: ‘We aren't talking about lawyers.’
Costello: ‘Then why talk about me?’

Detective Superintendent Jack Slipper, *of Scotland Yard, confronting fugitive Great Train Robber* **Ronnie Biggs** *in Rio de Janero:*

‘Hello Ronnie. Long time no see.’

Biggs: ‘Fuck me! How did you get here?’

Theodore 'The' Allen, *gangster, to a Congressional investigating committee:*

‘I am the wickedest man in New York.’

Congressman Rogers:

‘Allen is modest. He is the wickedest man in the world.’

First National Bank clerk, *during a raid by the Dillinger Gang, to a short man in a cap and brown overcoat:*

‘Hey you – get to work and notify somebody. The bank is being robbed.’

Baby Face Nelson, *looking at the machine gun he was pointing at her:*

‘Lady, you're telling me?’

Harry Pierpont *of the Dillinger gang, accused by a prosecutor of organising bank robberies that had netted $300,000:*

‘Well at least if I did, I'm not like some bank robbers - I didn't get myself elected president of the bank first.’

...later, to the same prosecutor:

‘I'm not the kind of man you are – robbing widows and orphans. You'd probably be like me if you had the nerve.’

Freddie Foreman:

‘People do get over familiar. I was at a boxing show and a guy said “Hi Fred, have you killed anyone lately?” I stopped and I just looked at him. I said, “The night's not over yet.”’

Arnold Rothstein, *New York gangster, to oil millionaire Colonel Henry Simms, a visitor to his gambling club:*

‘I hear you’re telling people that you’re a gambling man. How come you only play for chicken feed when you come to the Brook?’

Simms: ‘What do you call $60,000?’

Rothstein: ‘Chicken feed. I have a hundred thousand here. You match it and we’ll toss a coin for the money.’

Simms: ‘I never heard of such a thing.’

Rothstein, *pointing towards his stables:*

‘Next time you want to want to gamble, Colonel, try there.’

Christmas Humphreys, *prosecuting Donald Hume at the Old Bailey for the murder of Stanley Setty:*

‘I suggest that you stabbed Setty in the sitting-room and that he died in the dining-room...’

Hume: ‘Now you’re romancing!’

Humpheys then accused Hume...

‘And that you cut him up that night...’

Hume: ‘Absolute baloney!’

Donald Hume, *charged with murder in a Swiss court under the name Brown, asked by the judge if he was formerly known as Hume:*

‘You ask a silly question and you get a silly answer.’

Judge: ‘What is your name?’

Hume: ‘Don’t you know? You want to get a thicker pair of spectacles.’

...turning to the interpreter:

‘Tell that bum he should know who I am.’

Mr Justice Laws, *picking up on Michael Mansfield QC's use of the word 'analogise' in an IRA trial:*

'Is there such a word?'

Mansfield: 'There is, as a matter of fact.'

Laws: 'It is very inelegant.'

Mansfield: 'It comes of playing too much Scrabble.'

Judge Rogers, *to defence counsel William Rees-Davies QC, who arrived late and offered no explanation:*

'Mr Rees-Davies, don't you have something to say to me?'

Rees-Davies: 'Yes. Y'Lordship's clock's wrong. I meant to mention it yesterday but it slipped me mind.'

Peter Sutcliffe, *the Yorkshire Ripper, asked at his trial why he had try to cut the head off one of his victims:*

'Because she was in league with the Devil and between them they had hidden the £5 note and I was going to do the same thing with her head.'

Mr Justice Boreham: 'I don't want to get into a theological argument, but she and her colleague the Devil had beaten you and your God?'

Sutcliffe: 'Yes. It seemed so.'

Judge Bruce Laughland *had patiently explained to an Old Bailey jury in a City insider dealing case why he was directing them to acquit on certain charges. The clerk rose and said to the jury forewoman, 'On the judge's direction do you find the defendants guilty or not guilty of insider dealing?'*

Forewoman, *after a long pause:*

'Not sure.'

John Kelsey-Fry, cross examing bank robber
Noel 'Razor' Smith, *who had admitted previous convictions:*

❛Mr Smith, it is correct is it not, that your occupation is, in fact, as a member of the London underworld?❜

Razor Smith, *cupping hand to ear:*

❛The London Underground sir? No, I have never worked for them. I do have an uncle who works for British rail.❜

Jonathan Goldberg QC, *opening the defence at the Old Bailey in the marathon Brinks Mat robbery case:*

❛It is Day 71 of this trial. I feel like Barbara Hutton's seventh husband. I know what to do, it is how to make it interesting.❜

...to defendant, Brian Perry, in the same trial:

❛Please speak up, I am having difficulty hearing you.❜

Perry: ❛That's because you have got your wig over your ears.❜

A psychiatrist, giving evidence in the trial of **Jane Toppan***, the Massachusetts poisoner:*

‘She is suffering from a form of insanity that can never be cured.’

Toppan*, who had killed at least seventy people:*

‘The alienist lies. I am not crazy and all of you people know it.’

Arsenic Annie Doss*, asked by police about her fourth husband:*

‘I never heard of any Richard Morton.’

Police Officer: ‘What you don’t remember your previous husband?’

Doss: ‘Oh, that Richard Morton!’

Police Officer: ‘So you remember him?’

Doss: ‘Yes, I was married to him.’

Published letter in the Editor’s Postbag of crooked M.P. **Horatio Bottomley***’s* John Bull *magazine:*

‘A.LM. (Manchester) wants to know if the Editor has ever been incarcerated in one of HM Prisons? The answer is – not yet, but you never can tell.’

A prison visitor, noticing swindler and former Member of Parliament, **Horatio Bottomley***, sewing mailbags:*

‘Ah, Bottomley. Sewing, I see.’

Bottomley: ‘No sir, reaping.’

Michael West*, defence barrister, to* **Tony Wild***, supergrass:*

‘Must you loll like that in the witness box?’

Wild: ‘Must you loll like that when questioning?’

West: ‘Your evidence is vital. Everything else is worthless and so are you.’

Wild: ‘Yes. Yes. I’m a mad egotistical homosexual terrorist who wants to fit up these innocent people. Write it down.’

Mr Justice Eveleigh, *to* **Victor Durand**, *counsel in the Braintree Barn murder trial at Chelmsford Crown Court, who had told the court that he faced a long journey back to London on a slow train each evening:*

'What do you want me to do? Provide you with a brass band on the train?'

Durand: 'Even a jazz band would not speed up the journey - whatever the tempo.'

Illich Ramirez Sanchez, *better known as Carlos the Jackal, asked in a Paris court who he wanted as his advocate:*

'I hereby appoint Maitre Verges. Because he's a bigger terrorist than I am.'

Judge: 'I don't understand what he is referring to.'

Jacques Verges: 'Your honour, I believe he may be referring to my ideas.'

Judge Leo Glasser *to Mafia Don,* **John Gotti**, *who had made a gesture at his prosecutors:*

'If you can't refrain from doing that I will have you removed from the courtroom.'

Gotti: 'That's your prerogative. They don't need me to make gestures to describe them, for sure.'

Judge: 'Mr Gotti, I don't want to engage in any debate about this with you.'

Gotti: 'Neither do I. And I'm not here for a paycheck.'

Martin "Bugsy" Goldstein *of Murder Inc, noticing that the judge who was about to sentence him to death was wearing a hearing aid:*

'Before I die there is only one thing I would like to do - I would like to pee up your leg.'

Judge: 'Eh? What's that?'

Goldstein: 'I would like to pee up your leg.'

Judge: 'What's that he said?'

...the court clerk interpreted what Goldstein had said:

‘He said he would like to urinate on your honour’s trousers.’

Goldstein: ‘You cannot go to your death in a nice way. You might as well go in a bad way.’

Judge: ‘Having been tried and found guilty of murder in the first degree, the sentence is mandatory upon the court. The sentence of the court is that you be put to death...’

Goldstein: ‘In the electric chair.’

Judge: ‘...in the manner and in the place provided by law, during the week beginning November 4, 1940.’

Goldstein: ‘I will take it tomorrow and I will be satisfied.’

Francis ‘Two-Gun’ Crowley, *to the Warden of Sing Sing, as he was about to follow his partner-in-crime Rudolph ‘Fats’ Duringer to the electric chair:*

‘I got a favour to ask you.’

Warden: ‘Name it.’

Crowley: ‘I want a rag.’

Warden: ‘A rag? What for?’

Crowley: ‘I want to wipe the chair off after that rat sat in it.’

George Machine Gun Kelly *to con man, ‘Yellow Kid’ Weil, in Leavenworth Prison:*

‘I don’t understand a guy like you. You go right up to people and let ’em see your face. You go back time and time again to the same guy. What kind of crook are you?’

Weil: ‘The kind who’s doing a couple of years, George. I understand you’re doing life.’

Bernard Coy, *trying to interest fellow Alcatraz convict Clarence Carnes in an escape plot:*

‘How much time you doin’? Life?’

Carnes: ‘No. Ninety nine years.’

Dion O’Bannion, *to the police officer who caught him burgling a telegraph office with Hymie Weiss:*

‘Me and Hymie are waiting for the manager. We heard what good pay these telegraphers get and we wanted to sign on.’

Police officer: ‘What? You mean to tell me that you two fellas are in this office in the dark in the middle of the night to apply for jobs?’

O’Bannion: ‘That’s the very thing. You got to get up early to beat the other fella to the opportunities.’

Basil ‘The Owl’ Banghart, *defence witness in a Chicago kidnap trial of Roger Tuohy, to the prosecutor who had proved that he had not worked for three years:*

‘I had a steady job in 1931.’

Prosecutor: ‘Where?’

Banghart: ‘In the cotton duck mill in the US Penitentiary at Atlanta.’

Timmy Quilty, *winning the roll of dice that was to decide who would become new leader of New York’s White Hand Gang:*

‘I’m the boss!’

Wild Bill Lovett, *his rival, pulling a gun and shooting him:*

‘Now I’m the boss.’

Fear...

Al Capone:

‘You fear death every moment. Worse than death, you fear the rats of the game, who'd run and tell the police if you didn't constantly satisfy them with favours. I never was able to leave my home without a bodyguard.’

‘...I haven't had peace of mind in years. Even when I'm on a peace errand I take a chance on the light going suddenly out.’

Jack Ruby, *killer of Lee Harvey Oswald, appearing before the Warren Commission into the murder of John F. Kennedy:*

‘You dummies – can't you see that I can't tell it here? You people don't run this town. You can't protect me in Dallas. I'll get knifed in my cell and guards will be looking the other way.’

Leonardo Messina, *Sicilian mafioso:*

‘If you want to know if I worry about dying, I began to worry as soon as I joined. Everybody worries about dying in Sicily. Once the bosses used to die in their beds, now nobody dies in their beds anymore.’

Giovanni Falcone, *Sicilian Anti-Mafia magistrate, asked if he was ever afraid, shortly before he was murdered:*

‘I often reflect on a saying that strikes me – the courageous only die once; the scared die a thousand times a day.’

Gaspare Mutolo, *to Italy's Anti-Mafia Commission:*

‘What bothers us most is when you take our money away. We'd rather stay in jail and keep the money than be free without the money. That's the main thing.’

Eddie Guerin, *bank robber, on the courage required for villainy:*

‘Think of it, you people who lie in your bed of a night, and ask yourself whether you would like to go out at midnight for the purpose of dynamiting a safe, a job fraught with half a dozen disastrous possibilities. It is no use saying that crime doesn't require pluck and plenty of it. I know it does - the man doesn't breathe who can break into a place in the early hours of the morning without feeling the qualms of fear.’

Ronnie Knight, *on the customers at his London club:*

‘You could never afford to get too complacent with some of the ex-cons. Care and caution was the key phrase. Take a specimen like weedy Jimmy Essex. He wasn't much to look at. A bit like a balding garden gnome with no teeth and a pathetic mush. You had to feel sorry for him sometimes – but never enough to forget that he'd done a couple of murders.’

John Dickson, *former member of the Kray Firm:*

‘Most of us were loyal to the twins, mainly through fear of ending up on a marble slab.’

Jeffrey Archer, *in a melodramatic communication to his prison diary:*

‘They've now supplied me with a Bic razor and I consider cutting my throat. But the thought of failure is just too awful to contemplate.’

Hugh Collins, *former Glasgow gangster, who served a life sentence for murder:*

‘I have never taken part in a fight without the dread of being slashed or stabbed, of dying or being sent to prison. My legs used to shake, my stomach churned, my bowels were about to give way. I sweated profusely. No matter whom I faced I feared that I might come off second best, take a second prize...The physical actuality of the violence was a relief.’

Alan Decabriol, *whose evidence helped convict underworld figure Kenneth Noye of murder:*

‘I look over my shoulder every time I go into Sainsburys.’

Michael De Freitas, *known as Michael X:*

‘Killing is a strange thing. Before I killed for the first time I wondered if I would have a conscience. But I slept well and now I am no longer afraid.’

Big Jobs

Lucky Luciano:

‘Around 1925 I had a take of at least twelve million dollars from booze alone for the year. Naturally we didn’t pay no business taxes, like General Motors, but that didn’t mean that our expenses wasn’t pretty heavy.’

Ronnie Biggs, *recalling the feeling as he and his partners-in-crime counted the spoils of the Great Train Robbery:*

‘When the count reached £1 million we were invited to take a look at it, just so that we could have the pleasure of knowing what a million looked like. Charlie Wilson was dancing the twist, Gordon Goody singing the Gerry and the Pacemakers song *I Like It*... In fact all of us at that moment were behaving as if we hadn’t a care in the world.’

Tommy Wisbey, *another Great Train Robber:*

‘I think it would have been harder taking sweets off a baby.’

Bruce Reynolds, *on the hue and cry which followed:*

‘The heat was enormous. The daily papers were devoting page after page to the story, increasing pressure on the police. For their part, the Old Bill was throwing everything at the case – dozens of detectives, radio appeals, daily press briefings. Police were raiding as many as fifty addresses a day. You'd have thought we'd stolen the bloody Crown Jewels or massacred several busloads of senior politicians.’

James Saunders, *London solicitor:*

‘Most people lead extremely dull lives and the mere thought that someone has been able to burst out of here, grab a bag of wonga and have a good time is a great encouragement. Read the *Daily Mirror*. Myrtle Smith from Hartlepool won £10,000 in a bingo competition and is now going to get herself senseless drunk and go out with a gigolo and go on Concorde, this seems to be what it's all about. Most people lead such bloody awful lives that to know that at least hypothetically there are those who escape is uplifting. All the high moral tone about the train robbers is fairly pathetic.’

The Chief Constable of Durham, *explaining to a press conference in 1967 why he had surrounded Durham Prison with armed troops, after the arrival there of* **Gordon Goody** *and two other Great Train Robbers:*

‘I am satisfied that Goody's friends were prepared to launch something in the nature of a full-scale military attack, even to the extent of using tanks, bombs and what the Army describes as limited atomic weapons. Once armoured vehicles had breached the main gates there would be nothing to stop them. A couple of tanks could easily have come through the streets of Durham unchallenged. Nothing is too extravagant.❞

Valerio Viccei, *celebrating the £60million Knightsbridge Safe Deposit Co. Robbery in 1987:*

❝I reached for the golden tray and snipped a fragment off the huge rock of cocaine. I grabbed a platinum credit card belonging to some asshole with three family names and five titles just to cut myself a line of this beautiful stuff. Then I rolled a 1,000 Swiss franc bank note and zapped it in one go! I lay on my back again and took a long breath of pride and satisfaction. I rested my hands behind my head and said very quietly, "I did it!"❞

...explaining his motivation for the robbery:

❝What I have done is very serious. I will pay with my best years for this, but I do not repudiate my choices. Maybe I am a romantic lunatic who lives in his own world of dreams or fantasies. Money was the last thing on my mind. I was always waiting to reach something that was the top of its field.❞

Albert Spaggiari, *mastermind of the 1976 safe deposit robbery at the Societe Generale bank in Nice:*

❝I believe that any criminal act against a society is a political action. Most of all, robbery. But I don't mean petty theft which usually means picking the pockets of poor people. I mean Robbery. Now that's an art you've got to be born with.❞

Tom Keating, *art faker, who claimed that his copies of Samuel Palmer pictures were guided by the spirit of the artist himself:*

‘I’d sit in my little sketching room waiting for it to happen. I have never drawn a sheep from life but then Palmer’s sheep would begin to appear on the paper. Then Palmer’s “Valley of Vision Watched Over by the Good Shepherd in the Shadow of Shoreham Church”. With Sam’s permission I sometimes signed them with his own name, but they were his, not mine. It was his hand that guided the pen.’

Billy Hill, *London gangster, on the 1952 London mailbag robbery:*

‘Walk through Old Compton Street or down Wardour Street, or over the heath at Newmarket on any racing day, or along the promenade at Brighton any week, and ask anyone who thinks they know. Ask them who planned the Big Mailbag Job. The one when £287,000 in freely negotiable currency notes, in hard cash, was nicked, in May 1952, and they’ll all tell you. “We don’t know who did it but we’ve got a good idea. In any case we do know that Billy Hill planned it. Only he could have done that.”’

A police officer, *responding to pressure from Chicago church groups to close down the notorious twenty four bordello of the 1850s, known as Roger’s Barracks:*

‘Why, trying to close down those barracks would be like trying to arrest an elephant. There must be 200 armed men in there at all times.’

Carlos Lehder, *Columbian drug baron who revolutionised the narcotics trade by introducing high-tech equipment:*

‘I have bought and sold more aircraft than any other Latin American ever.’

Howard Marks, *jailed after being portrayed by the U.S. Drug Enforcement Authority as the world's biggest marijuana dealer:*

‘Talking to the snitches, I quickly discovered what small fry I really was. I had been charged with somehow being involved with a grand total of about a hundred tons of dope over a period of almost twenty years. Now I was associating with Cubans who had done more than that in a single shipment and had documentary evidence to prove it.’

Stefano Magaddino, *Canadian Mafia boss, on hearing that his rival, Joe Bonanno, had applied for Canadian citizenship:*

‘He's planting flags all over the world.’

Albert De Salvo, *the Boston Strangler, on his high sex drive:*

‘Five or six times a day don't mean much to me.’

Phil Kaufman, *on his old jail-mate, Charles Manson:*

‘I don't think he ever did physically murder anyone. He planted the seeds and other people did it. Charlie was too jail-smart to kill anybody. He may have cut off somebody's ear, but he was too smart to actually kill anybody. He did direct the thought traffic though.’

Nestor Alarcon, *Mexican peasant, on the fifty-five pesos he was paid to kill two people:*

‘That's a lot of money to a man like me.’

Chopper Read, *recalling the end of 1987, when he was jailed for burning down another drug-dealer's house, firing shots into the dealer's mother's home and shooting a criminal in the leg:*

'It was a busy few months.'

Albert Hattersley, *Northern safe-blower par excellence:*

'I've blown safes when there's been people asleep in the next room – and they never woke up.'

Dreams...

Reggie Kray:

‘My eventual aim is to be recognised first as a man and eventually as author, poet and philosopher.’

Ronnie Kray:

‘I knew from a very early age that I was going to kill someone. It was part of my destiny. And I always had this love of guns. I loved the feel of them, the touch of them and the sound they made when you fired them.’

Buster Edwards, *one of the Great Train Robbers:*

‘I dream sometimes of pulling off a really great job.’

Pittsburgh Phil Strauss, *hitman for Murder Inc., on his enthusiasm for his work:*

‘Like a ballplayer, that’s me. I figure I get seasoning doing these jobs here. Somebody from one of the big mobs spots me. Then, up to the big leagues.’

Bruce Reynolds, *mastermind of the Great Train Robbery:*

‘What I really liked about being a thief was every week you might find Eldorado.’

Jane Toppan, *Massachusetts nurse-cum-poisoner, annoyed because she could not recall all her seventy victims:*

‘I want to be known as the greatest criminal that ever lived. That is my ambition.’

John W. Dean, *convicted in the Watergate scandal:*

‘I wish I could write a book and not have to make a living.’

Frank Sinatra, *to fellow star Eddie Fisher:*

‘I’d rather be a don of the Mafia than President of the United States.’

Yoshio Kodama, *Japanese gangster, denying to a newspaper that he was a Yakusa boss:*

‘I would like to wash my hands of the worthless everyday world and enjoy my life fishing.’

Frank ‘The Mad Axeman’ Mitchell, *in a letter to* The Times *after escaping from Dartmoor and before he was murdered on the orders of Reggie and Ronnie Kray:*

‘I can only repeat my appeal to the humane thinking people of this country. If I must be buried alive give me some reason to hope.’

Dion O’Banion, *to a fellow gangster, after a profitable hi-jack:*

‘We’re big business without high hats.’

Al Capone:

"I have a wife and an eleven year old boy I idolize, at Palm Beach, Florida. If I could go there and forget it all I would be the happiest man in the world. I want peace, and I'm willing to live and let live. I'm tired of gang murders and gang shootings."

Carolyn Rothstein, *wife of Arnold, on the New York gangland boss's craving for money:*

"Until the end of the war he had money, but it was not too much for him to be able to count it. Afterwards there was so much of it he could not keep track of it. When we married, it was his ambition to have $100,000. Then he raised the limit, first to a quarter of a million, then to half a million and, finally, to a million. When he had his limit, he took off the limit. All he wanted was more."

Valerio Viccei, *on switching his attentions from terrorism to robbery:*

"I have abandoned the rarefied pure air of my idealised forest and travelled all the way down to the polluted town. I switched targets and instead of destabilising society, I long to make money just like its most respected citizens do."

Jean Belin, *French detective, on* **Jules Bonnot***'s band of anarchist robbers:*

"I have not the slightest doubt that in their warped minds they honestly thought they were about to light the spark that would set not only France but the whole world aflame, and in some undefined way bring about a new and better civilisation."

Aileen Wournos, *the first American convicted serial killer:*

‘I'm just waiting for Sherlock Holmes to crack this conspiracy wide open... I hope these no-good cops see prison in the future. I will seek to be electrocuted as soon as possible. I want to get off the fucking evil planet. I was a nice person, I've been treated like dirt...I just can't wait to leave. I'll be up in heaven when y'all are rotting in hell.’

Sam Giancana, *Mafia Godfather, speaking in the late 1950s:*

‘After Kennedy takes office and Castro gets hit, everybody in the country will have to come through me.’

...to his brother:

‘That's the problem with you, Chuck, you always wanna play it safe. Hey, that's OK, we're just different. You like runnin' a business. Me? I wanna run the country.’

John Christie, *the 10 Rillington Place murderer:*

‘For years I knew I had to kill just ten women, then my work would be finished.’

Charles Gervais, *killer of one of his prostitute girlfriend's clients, in a New Orleans television interview:*

‘In hell I will command souls. Legions of souls, ten thousand souls, all to rule over in hell. I'm going to torment them. I'm going to have them fight against God in the final war.’

A journalist *who visited thirty-three times killer,* **John Wayne Gacy**, *on Death Row:*

‘Gacy seemed unaware that he was in prison because he was a criminal. He seemed to think that I had come to see him because he was famous.’

Denis Nilsen, *to a colleague in the Civil Service, the evening before his arrest:*

‘If I am not in tomorrow I will be either ill, dead or in jail.’

Good Times, Bad Times

Jonathan Aitken, *former government minister jailed for perjury:*

‘Defeat, disgrace, divorce, bankruptcy and jail. Where did I screw up?’

Joe Cannon, *London villain, looking back:*

‘When middle-age puts a spare tyre round the guts, we all have thoughts about the good old days.’

Bruce Reynolds:

‘The wife's just been down the laundrette – hardly how people envisage the brain of the Great Train Robbery is living.’

Bill Gardner, *London villain of the Kray/Richardson era:*

‘We always wore suits, ties, collars. Today they're walking about with designer stubbles and dirty old shoes and you think – where's the pride gone?’

Ronnie Knight, *on the London of his youth:*

‘The East End was a safer place for ordinary folk in those days. Little old ladies could step out of a evening for a nice glass of stout down at the local without fear of having their heads bashed in. Now it's not safe for a prizefighter to be out after dark.’

Nipper Read, *policeman who arrested the Krays:*

‘People like Barbara Windsor and friends of the Krays fantasise about the very fact that they were around reduced crime. It’s absolute nonsense. She’s looking at Godfather Two.’

Nemone Lethbridge, *barrister who defended the Krays:*

‘Of course, to have a drink in a bar with Ronnie and Reggie at that time was rather like taking tea with Princess Margaret and Snowdon.’

Freddie Foreman, *Kray henchman:*

‘My old pal Alfie Gerrard used to say, when the Firm came up with problems: There’s nothing a few grand won’t cure.’

Jim Ridge, *former Garda, on crime in Dublin pre-1960s:*

‘People were so poor they had no time to go out stealing, they were simply trying to make a living. And they had nothing to steal. When I was a young officer, we dealt with gas-meter bandits. you would stop a boy in the street and sniff the coins in his pockets to try to smell the whiff of gas on them. If you wanted crime you had to go to the cinema and watch James Cagney say “Top of the world, Ma.”’

Jimmy O’Connor, *London villain-turned writer:*

‘The best thieves came from the East End, Hoxton, the Angel, the Elephant and Castle, and, of course, Notting Hill where they had a safe-blowing school. It’s thirty years now since I stole anything, but I still think like a thief; the thought of larceny is still there. I have larceny in my heart.’

Mad Frankie Fraser, *on being shot through the head in London in 1991:*

‘Whoever did shoot me, it was a complete botch-up. I know if things had been reversed and I had been doing the shooting they wouldn't have been alive. The gunman had to be a right mug, a right coward. He had it all his own way. He had me at his mercy and two point-blank shots completely missed. But it was good fun, good action, it makes a good night's drink after all.’

‘...You can't be lucky all the time. Take poor Wally Challis. He picked up ‘Dodger’ Mullins from Dartmoor after ‘Dodger’ finished a nine-year sentence and drove him back to London. On the way he knocked a man down and got five years. My luck wasn't as bad as that.’

‘...The War organised criminals. Before the War thieving was safes, jewellery, furs. Now a whole new world was opened up. there was so much money and stuff about – cigarettes, clothes, sugar, petrol coupons, anything. It was a thieves' paradise. I was a thief. Everyone was a thief.❜

Jack Spot, *London gangster of the 1950s:*

❛I didn't have to buy nothing. Every Jewish businessman in London made me clothes, give me money, food, drink, everything. Because I was a legend. I was what they call a legend to the Jews. Anywhere they had anti-semitic trouble – I was sent for: Manchester, Glasgow, anywhere. Some crook go into a Jewish shop, say gimme some clothes and a few quid, the local rabbi says go down London and find Jack Spot. Get Jack, he'll know what to do. So they did and I'd go up and chin a few bastards. The Robin Hood of the east End, a couple of taxi drivers told me once. "You helped everyone," they said.❜

...on a favourite method of maintaining gangland order:

❛I used to knock 'em out in the lavatory. That was my surgery. I used to go into the toilet and Bomp! Leave 'em in the piss.❜

Emmett Dalton, *last of the notorious Dalton brothers train robbery gang, in 1930 recalling the old days of the West:*

❛Men who killed other men, I observed, did not boast of it. They did not advertise their prowess, aggressive or defensive, by cutting a notch on a gun. It is a fiction writers' elaboration.❜

❛...In my time the lawless frontier was along the edge of the wilderness. Today the crime frontier is in the shadow of the skyscraper.❜

Al Capone, *on the crowd of photographers, newsmen and detectives present as he was escorted to the train taking him to prison:*

‘You'd think Mussolini was passing through.’

Willie Sutton, *refuting the story that, when one asked why he robbed banks he had said "That's where the money is":*

‘Why did I rob banks? Because I enjoyed it. I loved it. I was more alive when I was inside a bank, robbing it than at any other time in my life. I enjoyed everything about it so much that one or two weeks later I'd be out looking for the next job. But to me the money was the chips, that's all. The winnings. I kept robbing banks when, by all logic, it was foolish. When it could cost me far more than I could possibly gain.’

Razor Smith, *on a lifetime of armed robbery and imprisonment:*

‘We classed straight-goers as mugs and told each other stories about how we had outsmarted straight society, while sitting in top security prisons with real life passing us by. Who were the real mugs, I wondered?’

Donald 'Tony the Greek' Frankos, *hitman-cum-informer:*

‘I believe a major reason people drink or use drugs is because they enjoy it: booze and narcotics give pleasure or at least escape, and so too does the criminal life with its lack of stifling strictures and excellent income... If nothing else, my life was exciting: I knew it and I loved it.’

Peter Scott, *former cat burglar, recalling a job:*

❛The butler was laying a majestic table laden with food and silverware and I felt a bit like a missionary seeing my flock for the first time. I realised this was my life's work – persecuting the rich and the opulent.❜

Eddie Chapman, *retired safecracker:*

❛There was a hell of a depression hitting the country, but we lived like multi-millionaires. The one thing we had was money. Whenever we ran out we used to go out and blow another safe... Life was a bit fast and furious then.❜

Billy Hill, *on the profits of wartime crime:*

‘Money? It was coming to us like pieces of dirty paper. I rarely went out with less than a monkey or a grand in my pocket. That was spending stuff. Emergency funds in case I got nicked or in case the bite was put on me.’

Nipper Read, *the policeman who arrested the Krays, on the 1950s:*

‘Society was different, crime was different, villains were different. Villains gave themselves up, villains pleaded guilty.’

Henry Hill – **Wiseguy** – *on his childhood among the Mafia hoods of New York City:*

‘I was the luckiest kid in the world. People like my father couldn't understand, but I was part of something. I belonged. I was treated like I was a grown-up. I was living a fantasy. Wiseguys would pull up and toss me their keys and let me park their Caddies. I couldn't see over the steering wheel and I'm parking Caddies.’

Pittsburgh Phil Strauss, *advising his Murder Inc. partner, Happy Maione, on how to leave the scene of a killing:*

‘We're just a coupla visitors to the fair city of Detroit, Hap. Come to see the new cars and the big factories. Yeah, that's us. Tourists. That guy back there shot full of holes? Hell, we don't know a thing about it. Maybe it was the local boys, the Purple gang, you know? Sure, the cops will be looking for the locals, that guy's real enemies, people he knows. Not us, never us, we're strangers in town just looking for a good time.’

Reggie Woolmington, *on hearing that his conviction for killing his wife – and his death sentence – had been quashed by the House of Lords:*

‘It's great to light a pipe again, but I shall miss my wife.’

Joe Cannon, *London villain, looking back in the early '80s on his time in Dartmoor Prison:*

‘Some events stand out in my memory. The picture of Bobby Ramsey, ex-boxer and an associate of Billy Hill, serving seven for a bloody attack on Terry Martin in 1956 is as fresh in my mind as though it were yesterday. He had suddenly got religious and marched round the touchline at the Saturday football game calling on God for help and guidance. It couldn't be anything but a joke. "Turn it in Bobby," said one of the spectators. "You might kid the chaplain but you can't kid God. He can see through you."

The angel of light, love and mercy turned on the doubting Thomas and knocked him spark out with a right-hander that spread the poor fellow's nose all over his face. This smiting of the philistine went unnoticed by all but a few of those standing nearby. Perhaps it was even too quick for God to see.’

George Ince, *who was tried twice for the Braintree Barn murder, which he did not commit, recalling his feelings on picked out at an identification parade:*

‘I could have fallen through the floor. I could have collapsed when they touched me on the shoulder. I wanted to protest, to tell them that it wasn't true, but the words wouldn't come out.’

Arthur Harding, *turn-of-the-century East End villain, on a contemporary:*

'Greeny was a scoundrel. The kind who would stick a knife into your back without warning. He terrorised Hoxton. His uncle was a terror and all. The police in G Division hated the sight of him, because he was always knocking coppers about. Greeny couldn't thieve for toffee. He was no-gooder, a scrounger. But he ran off with a shopkeeper's wife. Lovely woman she was, with beautiful blond hair. Well she went for an outing to Southend and she met this bleeding tike in a pub, and she left her family, her home, her husband and everything for him. Forsaking everything to live with this bloody tike who never earned a bleeding penny in his life.'

Charlie Kray:

'Women say to me, In those days I used to go out day and night. Now I don't go out after 3 o'clock, but when they were about I could go out at 2 o' clock in the morning... And all the people would help you across the road and say Are you all right? Do you want anything? You could leave your doors open. No one broke into your house. But now, well it's terrible. It's a terrible old world.'

Jonathan King, *music mogul in jail for buggery:*

'Friends say I'm putting a brave face on it – bollocks – this is far and away the most stimulating, fascinating thing that's ever happened to me.'

Edward Bunker, *who played Mr Blue in the movie* Reservoir Dogs *and is an acclaimed novelist:*

‘I turned 18 in San Quentin. It’s not some country club – I didn’t smile for a couple of years.’

Chopper Read:

‘You walk through the shadow of the valley of death and you try to get to the other end alive. Very few people make it. The one who wins the game is the one who lives the longest.’

Peter Scott, *former cat-burglar:*

‘I have no money but I have retained my arrogance. I am not reformed, I just have no more time to offer them, no more of my life to give them behind bars, so I have stopped. There was no road to Damascus, no burning bush, I simply didn’t fancy getting locked up again.’

Tiny Mazzanars

of the Chicago Bookie Gang, on where the money went:

‘Dice, horses, women got everything we made – mostly dice.’

Canaries, Grasses and Stool Pigeons

Peter Bleksley, *former Scotland Yard detective:*

‘Call them what you like – squealer, grass, snitch, nark, snout – it's a fact of life that the police can't do without them. They are the bread and butter, the inescapable mainstay of the undercover work I was involved in...a necessary evil in the battle against crime. At the same time, I have no hesitation in describing them as the utter, total, pits of the earth. And I reckon I'm more qualified than anyone to say that because I've worked with hundreds, most of them utter scum.’

Nutty Sharpe, *former head of Scotland Yard's Flying Squad, on the need for informers:*

‘It's no use going to the Plymouth Brotherhood to find out about crime.’

Albert Spaggiari, *French master criminal:*

‘Without stool pigeons, there wouldn't be any arrests. the day robbers get together and eliminate all the squealers, the Police Nationale might just as well close up shop. All that business about brilliant deductions and relentless sleuthing – that's a lot of crap straight out of some comic book.’

Charles Kray:

❛I understand the need for the police to have informers, but it seems to me that they are trying to make a nation of them. In the long term, we will have a nation of traitors.❜

Albert Donaghue, *member of the Kray gang who turned Queen's Evidence against them:*

❛So this fine pair were our leaders. Hardly inspirational – nothing like Robin Hood, Napoleon or Nelson – not the kind of people you would go over the top and die for. Except that, rather like those poor sods who did die for mad generals in World War I, few of us had any choice. If we refused to do what they wanted, we could have been shot.❜

William Murphy, *who, although himself on remand for a £10,000 contract murder, gave evidence against fellow prisoner John Bindon:*

❛I don't think it's right people should go around killing other people and getting paid for it.❜

Joe Valachi, *Mafia informer:*

❛All I did was try to protect myself...I hope the American people will benefit by knowing what the mob is like. If I was killed in Atlanta I would have died branded as a rat anyway, without doing anything wrong. So what did I lose?❜

...explaining why Salvatore Maranzano, founder of the modern U.S. Mafia, sat on a throne underneath a large cross when presiding over a meeting of five hundred gangsters:

❛He had done this so that if outsiders wondered what the meeting was about, they would think we belonged to some kind of holy society.❜

Luis 'Kojak' Garcia, *American drug dealer-turned informer:*

‘When you play, you pay.’

Tommaso Buscetta, *Sicilian Godfather of Two Worlds, who gave evidence against hundreds of mafiosi after members of his family were murdered:*

‘I am not an informer. I am not a supergrass. I was a mafioso and I am responsible for crimes for which I am ready to pay my debt to justice.’

‘This is not revenge for my family's death. Revenge for my family's death would have been to go and kill their sons: it's not even close. I don't want revenge – I want to destroy the Mafia, I want to reveal it for what it is, what it has become...a criminal organisation with no other purpose.’

‘...It's necessary to know who I am. I'm a normal person but Mother Nature gave me charisma. I have something extra...I'm a very authoritative figure in Cosa Nostra, They come looking for me when there are difficult questions to settle, because if I pronounce an opinion, it's the right one, and they'll be forced to admit, "Tommaso said this."’

Raymond Gilmour, *RUC informer, on Cathal 'Drummer' Crumley, Sinn Fein by-election candidate:*

‘My special branch handler used to give me money to buy "Drummer" drink and pump him for information on the IRA. Three or four pints and he would tell you anything.’

Tony Wild, *supergrass, asked while giving evidence in court if he was a homosexual:*

‘I have been to bed with literally hundreds of women and I could call five hundred into this court to testify to that fact. I have also had dozens of jobs of a masculine nature. I cannot bear men touching me. My crimes, I know, have got progressively more serious, ending up with armed robbery. I would interpret that as an attempt or, at least, a sub-conscious attempt to regain my manhood.’

Bertie Smalls, *charged with a series of armed robberies on London banks and looking at a very lengthy prison sentence:*

‘I want to give Queen's Evidence, just give me a guarantee. I can give you every robber in London.’

Defence barrister *at the Old Bailey to supergrass,* **Bertie Smalls***:*

‘I don't want to be offensive but you've been many things in your time. Thief. Bank robber. Ponce. I am suggesting you are now a liar.’

A document headed 'Press Release', smuggled into court before **Bertie Smalls** *was about to give Queen's Evidence against his former associates – who had allegedly taken out a contract on him:*

‘Mr Bertie Smalls, the famous solo singer, who recently broke away from the Home Counties Choral Society, is about to give up the singing side of his career. Apparently Mr Smalls feels that the singing may affect his throat - permanently. When interviewed on Wednesday Mr Smalls refused to comment.’

Sammy 'The Bull' Gravano, *giving evidence against John Gotti:*

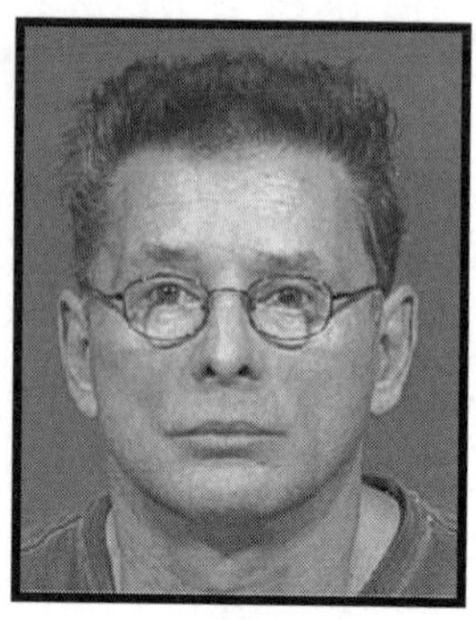

‘Sometimes I was a shooter, sometimes I was a back-up shooter. Sometimes I set the guy up. Sometimes I just talked about it.’

Henry Hill, *Mafia informer whose life was turned into the film* Goodfellas*:*

‘The hardest thing for me was leaving the life I was running away from. Even at the end, with all the threats I was getting and all the time I was facing behind the wall, I still loved the life... We walked in a room and the place stopped. Everyone knew who we were, and we were treated like movie stars with muscle. We had it all and it was all free. Truckloads of swag. Fur coats, TVs, clothes – all for the asking. We used Jimmy's hijack drops like department stores. Our wives, mothers, kids, everybody rode along. I had paper bags filled with jewellery stashed in the kitchen and a sugar bowl full of coke next to the bed. Anything I wanted was only a phone call away. Free rented cars under phony names and keys to a dozen hideout apartments we shared. I would bet thirty and forty grand over a weekend and then I would blow the winnings in a week or go to the sharks to pay back the bookies. It didn't matter. When I was broke I just went out and robbed some more. We ran everything. We paid the lawyers. We paid the cops. Everybody had their hands out. we walked out laughing. We had the best of everything. In Vegas and Atlantic City somebody always knew someone. People would come over and offer us shows, dinners, sweets. And now that is all over, and that's the hardest part. Today everything is very different. No more action. I have to wait around like everyone else. I'm an average nobody – I get to live the rest of my life like a schnook.❜

Donald 'Tony the Greek' Frankos,
contract killer to the Mafia, on turning informer:

❛All my life I've hated rats. I can't believe I became one. I wake up in my cell at night and think, you're a rat, nothing but a lowdown rat. That bothers me more than any other thing I've ever done in my life. I went for their bullshit. Me, Mr Street Smart, and I went for it like a stone sucker. I guess I'm sorry for all the guys I killed, but for the most part they were scumbags. Now John Gotti, John's offered three hundred thousand dollars to anyone who hits the Greek. Gotti was my friend. It makes me more sad than scared. My old friends gone, my self-respect gone. My manhood gone. I was the last person anyone thought would rat.❜

Albert Anastasia, *the Mafia killer, seeing a witness to the arrest of bank robber Willie Sutton (whom he did not know) interviewed on television:*

‘I can't stand squealers! Hit that guy!’

...and he was.

Maurice O'Mahoney, *self-styled 'King Squealer' who betrayed two hundred of his former associates in the London underworld:*

‘If I had to do it all again I'd still do what I did for the law. The British police have taught me a hell of a lot and now I am on their side all the way. And I hope that by my actions I have at least saved some lives. Though whether I've saved my own is highly questionable.’

...later, after his police protection was withdrawn:

‘They've dropped me flat, the canary that fell from its cage. They've told me to go out and get a decent job. The only trade I know is how to break into banks. I'm in a terrible state. I could go round the corner and cry.’

Jimmy Fratianno, *Mafia informer, on the likelihood of those he betrayed catching up with him:*

‘I just take my chances, go some place where they can't find me, just live as long as I can. It's better than being dead. You know, when they find you: "Bye Bye Baby!" What are you gonna do? But let them find me. If I had stayed on with them I would have been dead already, right? So every day I'm still living I beat them!"

Ronald Brown, *claiming that he would not have turned informant if his friends had got him out of prison:*

"If they'd sprung me on the second or third day, I probably would have stayed a burglar."

Vincent Teresa, *Mafia informer:*

"You can hope and pray for a lot but a guy like myself has to face up to the fact that as long as I live, the mob will hunt me. They won't forget. They can't. They have to prove to others that one guy can't get away with what I did and still live. Maybe they're right. I hope not."

Lawrence 'The Snake' Cain, *on his standing in the underworld after becoming an informer:*

"No one will come near me unless it is to kill me."

Regrets...?

Jack Ruby, *on his motive for shooting Lee Harvey Oswald:*

‘All I wanted to do was be a hero and it looks like I fucked things up.’

Sirhan Sirhan, *at the suggestion he could have been out of control or insane when he shot Senator Robert Kennedy:*

‘I'd rather die and say I killed the son of a bitch.’

Machine Gun Kelly, *writing from Leavenworth Prison shortly before his death in 1954:*

‘These five words seem written in fire on the walls of my cell – *Nothing can be worth this*. This – the kind of life I am leading. This is the final word of wisdom so far as crime is concerned.’

Charles Manson:

‘I am not ashamed or sorry. If it takes fear and violence to open the eyes of the dollar-conscious society, the name Charles Manson can be that fear.’

Sam Giancana, *on murder:*

‘Seven out of ten times when we hit a guy, we're wrong. But the other three times we hit, we make up for it.’

Jimmy 'The Weasel' Fratianno, *on killing people:*

❛I didn't have much feeling because I never killed nobody that was innocent. They were all gangsters, they were killers themselves. It might bother me if I killed an innocent person, somebody that didn't deserve it. Guys that I fooled with, they were out to kill us. I couldn't kill a woman, innocent people, kids. I couldn't do that.❜

Charles Sobraj, *Vietnamese gems dealer, after murdering eight tourists in Thailand:*

❛If some will ask me whether I feel remorse – and many will – I answer: Does a professional soldier feel remorse after having killed a hundred men with a machine gun? Did the American pilots feel remorse after dropping napalm on my homeland? No. Society condoned the soldiers, telling them: You have the right to kill; it is your duty to kill – the more you kill the bigger the promotion. Don't I have the same right? In the interests of my own minority?❜

Michael Ryan, *the Hungerford Killer, to a police officer, after the massacre and shortly before shooting himself in the head:*

❛I should have stayed in bed.❜

Ian Brady, *Moors Murderer:*

❛I'm not interested in verbal hairshirts, sackcloth and ashes.❜

Frank Kidnew, *slashed more than a hundred times about the body in the Sheffield gang wars of the 1920s:*

❛I reckon they've spoiled my suit.❜

Christy Dunne, *of the Dublin criminal family, recalling his youth:*

‘I never thought of reforming, I just wanted to rob and achieve a sense of importance.’

Charlie Peace, *on having shot two men dead:*

‘My greatest mistake,sir, has been this: in all my career I have used ball cartridges. I ought to have used blanks.’

Paul Castellano, *Boss of Bosses, to the FBI agents who arrested him:*

‘Bugging a man's house – I'm sorry fellas, I know you got your job to do, but I don't think that's right. Place of business, okay. Social club, alright. But a man's home? It's personal. No one needs to know what a man says or does when he's home. I'm sure you know all sorts of things about me that no one really has the right to know.’

Meyer Lansky, *Mafia don, to reporters after an appearance before a grand jury:*

‘I don't want to spoil the drama of your stories. So I don't think I'll say anything.’

Klondike O'Donnell, *of the West Side Chicago gang, on fellow gangster James 'Fur' Sammons:*

‘A good killer, but unreliable. We'll have to bump him off.’

Don Calogero Vizzini, *Sicilian godfather, expressing regret towards the end of his life at the deterioration in the Mafia's code of honour:*

‘When I die, the Mafia dies.’

Razor Smith, *jailed London robber:*

‘When I was a kid all my heroes were criminals - Jesse James, Robin Hood, John Dillinger, John McVicar and the Great Train Robbers. I was always fascinated by people like that and so as soon as I could I wasted no time in getting myself into a life of crime. I've spent half my life trying to emulate my heroes and all along I've missed the point. Half of them ended up shot dead in the street and the other half ended up doing bundles of bird – with the exception of Robin Hood... who must have had a blinding brief!’

Bruce Reynolds, *mastermind of the Great Train Robbery, reflecting on contemporary criminal trends:*

‘Drugs change it all. Up until the train I'd had various large chunks of money and I was more or less on the pinnacle. There wasn't anyone getting packets and packets. Today they're fetching in a million pounds worth of dope every day. There's so much money and you don't need an awful lot of skill. It's not like an adventure – it's business!’

Ellis Lincoln, *after being struck off as a solicitor:*

‘I feel I should be like my train-robber client, Thomas Wisbey. I should sit on a boiler-house roof and protest.’

Taters Chatham, *retired burglar:*

‘What have I got? A lot of sad memories. And thirty years inside.’

Charlie Richardson, *South London gangleader of the 1960s:*

‘In 1966 when I was in court the country appeared to be filled with indignation and moral outrage. If my trial had been in 1986 instead of ‘66 I would have employed a PR and marketing company to syndicate me. There would have been “Charlie Richardson is innocent” T-shirts and “Teenage Mutant Charlie Boy the Torture Gang Boss” cuddly toys for kids at Christmas.’

George Blake, *spy, whose escape from a 42 year sentence at Wormwood Scrubs led to the introduction of maximum security in British prisons:*

‘I am sadly aware that my escape has been the immediate cause of a serious worsening of the conditions in which inmates, and especially those among them who have been sentenced to very long terms, are kept...I am deeply sorry about this.’

William Shaw, *John Dillinger's first professional partner in crime, looking back in later years:*

‘Guess I was borned to be a hoodlum. I have lived a life of crime and misery and wouldn't take a fortune for my experience. Rest assured it's nothing to be proud of. Thirteen months freedom in the last twenty-eight years – it's not very glamorous, is it?’

Lucky Luciano, *asked shortly before his death in 1962 whether, if he had the chance, he would live his life the same way:*

‘I'd do it legal. I learned too late that you need just as good a brain to make a crooked million as an honest million. These days, you apply for a licence to steal from the public. If I had my time again I'd make sure I got that licence first.’

Heidi Fleiss, *jailed Hollywood brothel-keeper:*

‘I miss the days when I could reach under my bed and pull out half a million dollars in cash.’

Execution

Michael Durocher, *convicted murderer, writing to the Governor of Florida begging him to sign the death warrant:*

‘I am a believer in capital punishment and I respectfully request that justice be done.’

Fred Lusk, *lawyer for Donald Leroy Evans, who murdered sixty people across America:*

‘He said he lived by the sword and he wants to die by the sword, he does not believe in suicide so he wants to die by execution. I’ll help him with everything, all his wishes, but it goes against my legal ethics to plead him to death.’

Caryl Chessman, *who spent twelve years on Death Row at San Quentin before going to the gas chamber in 1960:*

‘I have had nine execution dates and have been spared eight times. I do not want to be credited with more lives than a cat.’

Ruth Ellis, *the last woman to be hanged in Britain, when told of the many people campaigning for a reprieve:*

‘I am very grateful for them. But I am quite happy to die.’

‘...I won’t go to prison for ten years and come out old and finished. I’d rather be hanged.’

Justice Heath, *the 18th Century hanging judge who ordered the death penalty in all capital cases (over 200), claiming that he knew of no other adequate punishment:*

‘If you imprison at home, the criminal is soon thrown upon you again hardened in crime. If you transport, you corrupt infant societies and sow the seeds of atrocious crimes over the habitable globe. There is no regenerating of felons in this life and for their own sakes, as well as for the sake of society, I think it is better to hang.’

John Hadfield, *18th Century impostor sentenced to death for fraud and seduction, as he arrived on the scaffold:*

‘Oh happy sight, I see it with pleasure.’

Donald ‘Tony the Greek’ Frankos, *hitman-cum-informer:*

‘Gangster films of the thirties and forties took millions of movie-goers up the river with James Cagney, Edward G. Robinson, George Raft, and Humphrey Bogart for an inside look at the Big House at Sing Sing. Hollywood always dramatized some poor sap being dragged kicking and screaming to the electric chair, his pleas for mercy drowned out by the melancholy wail of a harmonica or an old black man humming a tear-jerking tune in the background. That was all bullshit.’

Fritz Haarman, *mass murderer of Hanover:*

‘I want to pass just one more merry evening in my cell, with coffee, cheese and cigars, after which I will curse my father and go to my execution as if it were a wedding.’

Richard Ramirez, *the Night Stalker, after being sentenced to death in California:*

“Big deal – death always went with the territory. I’ll see you in Disneyland.”

Official instructions to Frank Hamer, *the Texas Ranger given the task of hunting down Bonnie and Clyde:*

“Put them on the spot, know you’re right and shoot everything in sight.”

Gary Gilmore, *to an informer in prison:*

“They’re figuring to give me the death penalty but I have an answer for that…I’m going to make them do it. Then we’ll see if they have as much guts as I do.”

Charles Becker’*s demise in the electric chair, when three separate jolts of electricity, each ten seconds long and 1850 volts strong were required to kill him, as described by a witness:*

“To those who had sat in the gray-walled room and watched and listened to the rasping sound of the wooden switch lever being thrown backward and forward and had seen the greenish-blue blaze at the victim’s head and feet, and the grayish smoke curling away from the scorched flesh, it had seemed an hour.”

Executioners...

Dr Joseph-Ignace Guillotin, *inventor of the guillotine, describing his beheading device to the French National Assembly in 1789:*

‘The mechanism falls like lightning; the head flies off; the blood spurts; the man no longer exists. Gentlemen, with my machine I'll take off your head in a flash and you won't even feel the slightest pain.’

Albert Pierrepoint, *after retiring as public hangman:*

‘I do not now believe that any of the hundreds of executions I carried out has in any way acted as a deterrent against future murder. Capital punishment, in my view, achieved nothing except revenge.’

...recalling his first execution:

‘A dead man, being taken down from execution, is a uniquely broken body whether he is a criminal or Christ and I received this flesh, leaning helplessly into my arms, with the linen round the loins, gently with the reverence I thought due to the shell of any man who has sinned and suffered.’

...on the need for a conscientious attitude towards hanging people:

‘On the actual job you’re dealing with human flesh. You’ve got to get it right.’

‘...I operated on behalf of the State, what I am convinced was the most humane and the most dignified method of meting out death to a delinquent.’

James Berry, *shoe salesman-turned-hangman, claiming that, as he had ‘served under four Home Secretaries’, his position should be salaried and with a pension:*

‘It seems a horrible thing that I should have to peruse newspaper reports in the hope that a fellow-creature may be condemned to death, whenever I wish to feel sure that business is not “falling off”.’

Louis Deibler, *French executioner of the 19th Century, replying to a critic who complained that he was too slow in operating the guillotine:*

‘I’d like to see you there. I have no desire to have two or three fingers eaten by the blade.’

Saeed Al Sayaf, *Saudi Arabia’s official executioner, who in 1989 claimed to have chopped off 600 heads:*

‘To chop off the heads of men I use a special sword, following the writings of the Prophet Mohammed, while I use a gun to execute women. The reason for using the gun is to avoid removing any part of the cover on the upper part of a woman’s body. When the job is done I get a sense of delight ... and I thank God for giving me this power.’

...speaking in 2003:

‘Two, four, ten – as long as I’m doing God’s will it doesn’t matter how many I execute.’

... speaking about the sword he uses to execute people:

‘It’s a gift from the Government. I look after it and sharpen it once in a while and I make sure to clean it of bloodstains. People are amazed how fast it can separate the head from the body.’

‘...There are many people who faint when they witness an execution. I don’t know why they come and watch if they don’t have the stomach for it. Me? I sleep very well.’

Al-Basri, a sport physician for 16 years was **Saddam Hussein***’s personal trainer:*

‘One minute he was all gentle, mild as a poet and the next he was like a beast...Once this woman came in, kissing his hands and feet. Her husband was in prison and she was begging for his release. He smiled at her, wrote out a note for some money to be given to her and said her husband would be back home the next day. When the woman had left, Saddam turned to his security adviser, “He's still alive then?” he asked. To which came the reply that the man had not yet been sentenced for his crime. Saddam said, “Well, I gave her my word that he would be home tomorrow, so kill him and send her the body” He was laughing as he said it.’

Tom Pierrepoint, *public hangman, speaking of a rival, John Ellis:*

‘If I ever meet Ellis I’ll kill him – it doesn’t matter if it is in the church.’

...to his nephew Albert, on hearing that Ellis had attempted suicide by shooting himself in the head:

‘He should have done it bloody years ago. It was impossible to work with him.’

John Ellis, *hangman, on the sense of isolation that his job brought:*

‘Conversations cease suddenly when I am about and I can feel people eyeing me as if I am some exhibit in the chamber of horrors. They will avoid shaking hands with me when they are introduced – they shudder at the idea of grasping the hand that has pinioned murderers and worked the gallows lever. Socially it is a bad business being a hangman.’

...on the insecurity of the hangman's job:

‘Hangmen are not paid as they ought to be and there is no pension...I have been as long as nine months without an execution to deal with. I had to carry on another business – I am a barber – because there was not a living in it.’

William Marwood, *19th-Century hangman, to his victims:*

‘Please don't hold this against me. I'm only doing my duty. I'll try and make it as painless as possible.’

‘...When I tap a prisoner on the shoulder, he nearly always comes to me.’

...on the hanging of Charlie Peace:

‘I expected difficulties because he was such a desperate man, but bless you my dear sir, he passed away like a summer's eve.’

...speaking derisively of his predecessor William Calcraft:

'He hanged them. I execute them.'

...to a bystander who asked him why he did not hang his dog, which was on its last legs:

'No, no. Hang a man, but my dear old dog, never!'

Syd Dernley, *Britain's last hangman:*

'I was a professional and I wanted to achieve the fastest hanging ever. I did one chap in seven seconds. They should place that in the *Guinness Book of Records.*'

Tom Pierrepoint, *foreseeing the abolition of his trade:*

'There'll come a bloody day when they'll all be reprieved.'

Last Words...

Charlie Peace, *to the prison chaplain, shortly before he went to the gallows:*

‘What is the scaffold? A short cut to Heaven.’

...to a warder:

‘You’re in a hell of a hurry. Who’s going to be hanged this morning, you or me?’

Henri Landru, *French serial killer, asked by a priest if he wished to make a last confession on his way to the guillotine:*

‘I am very sorry, but I must not keep these gentlemen waiting.’

Gerald Chapman, *about to be hanged in Connecticut for murdering a prison guard:*

‘Death itself isn’t dreadful, but hanging seems an awkward way of entering the adventure.’

Gary Gilmore, *as he stood, hooded, before a firing squad and was asked if he had anything he would like to say:*

‘Let’s do it.’

Black Jack Ketchum *on the gallows in New Mexico, 1901, to spectators gathered below:*

‘I’ll be in hell before you start breakfast boys. Let her rip.’

Edgar Edwards, *murderer, as he walked to the scaffold at Wandsworth in 1903:*

‘I’ve been looking forward to this a lot.’

Kenneth Neu, *double murderer who, wearing a suit belonging to one of his victims, grinned and tossed coins as he was sentenced to death, then tap danced on Death Row and sang on the gallows:*

‘I’m as fit as a fiddle and ready to hang.’

Carl Panzram, *robber and murderer, asked by the hangman if he had anything to say:*

‘Yes, hurry it up you hoozier bastard. I could hang a dozen men while you’re fooling around.’

Neville Heath, *the Acid Bath Killer, accepting the hangman’s offer of a glass of whisky as he walked to the scaffold:*

‘You might as well make that a double.’

Thomas McGuiness, *Scottish murderer, offered a tot of brandy by the hangman:*

‘I have been a teetotaller all my days and I’ll manage without it now.’

Charles Avinain, *French mass murderer, asked as he stood awaiting the guillotine blade if he had any last words:*

‘Never confess!’

Black Jack, *Australian bushranger, as he stood on the scaffold and was urged by a chaplain to pray:*

‘Pray yourself – I’m too frightened.’

Musquito, *the ‘Black Napoleon’, aborigine bushranger, as he was about to be hanged for murder in 1825:*

‘Hanging’s no good for black fellow. All right for white fellow, they used to it.’

Charles Birger, *Illinois murderer, to his guards, as he surveyed the crowd who had gathered to watch his hanging:*

‘Never did see so many ugly people in my life. They're no better looking than you fellows.’

Marcel Petiot, *to official witnesses as he was about face the guillotine:*

‘Gentlemen, I ask you not to look. This will not be pretty.’

Dr William Palmer, *Victorian mass murderer, as he stood on the gallows at Stafford Jail:*

‘Are you sure this thing is safe?’

Jules Bonnot, *leader of the Motor Bandits, a French anarchist gang of bank robbers, as he lay dying after being shot by the police:*

‘I am famous now. My fame has spread throughout the world. For my part I could have done without this kind of glory. I have tried to live my own kind of life and I have a right to live.’

John Owen, *Wolverhampton-born tramp, to journalists shortly before his execution for the murder of a village blacksmith:*

‘My friends, I am about to suffer for the death of – let me see! What was the name? Oh, Emmanuel Marshall. But, my friends, I am innocent!’

Claude Buffet, *the last person to be executed by guillotine in France:*

‘The man that I am wants to die by the guillotine. Let it be known that Claude Buffet commits suicide by the guillotine.’

Dr Neill Cream, *a suspect in the Jack the Ripper investigation, as he was hanged in 1892 for a separate murder:*

'I am Jack...'

Frederick Seddon, *informed the night before his execution that his house had been sold for less than its market value:*

'That's finished it!'

Anton J. Cermak, *to Franklin D. Roosevelt, as he fell dying from an assassin's bullet intended for the President-elect:*

'I'm glad it was me and not you.'

Dutch Schultz, *Chicago gangster, as he lay dying from gunshot wounds in 1935:*

'Please put me up on my feet at once! You are a hard-boiled man. Did you hear me? I would hear it, the circuit Court would hear it and the Supreme Court might hear it. If that ain't the payroll. Please crack down on the Chinaman's friends and Hitler's commander. I am sore and I am going up and I am going to give you honey, if I can. Mother is the best bet and don't let Satan draw you too fast.'

Arnold Rothstein, *New York gangster to a policeman as he was dying of gunshot wounds,:*

'I'm not talking. You stick to your trade and I'll stick to mine.'

Frank Gusenberg, *victim of the St. Valentine's Day Massacre, as he lay dying with fourteen machine gun bullets in his body:*

'Nobody shot me.'

Gus Wernicke, *the youngest bushranger in Australian history, after being shot by the police:*

'Oh God I'm shot and I'm only fifteen!'

William Kemmler, *the first man in the USA to go to the electric chair, to witnesses:*

‘The newspapers have been saying a lot of things about me which were not so. I wish you all good luck in the world. I believe I am going to a better place.’

...to the sheriff who was adjusting the straps:

‘Don't get excited Jim. I want you to make a good job of this.’

William Deni, *Philadelphia police killer, as he was strapped into the electric chair:*

‘I guess the Big Bad Wolf is going to get me.’

Charles Fithian, *shortly before he was electrocuted in New Jersey:*

‘I want to make a complaint. The soup I had for supper tonight was too hot.’

George Appel, *Chicago gunman, grinning at witnesses as he was being strapped into the electric chair:*

‘Well folks, you'll soon see a baked Appel.’

Dr. Arthur Warren Waite *to a warder as he was strapped into the chair at Sing Sing:*

‘Is this all there is to it?’

Michael Sclafoni, *running a finger over the arm of the electric chair:*

‘Dust! They at least could give a man about to die a clean chair!’

Donald ‘Pee Wee’ Gaskins, *serial killer, shortly before he went to the electric chair in 1991:*

‘I've gotten a lot of letters over the years from

Satan-Worshippers who want my corpse. Some have even wrote and told me that if I don't leave my body to them legally, in my Last Will and Testament, they will find out where I am buried and dig me up. They say they want my corpse because it will have special Powers of Evil on account of all the people I killed; and every year on the anniversary of my execution, they want to hold a Black mass in my name, to honour my memory and remind the world who I was...I have walked the same path as God. By taking lives and making others afraid of me, I become God's equal. Through killing others I have become my own Master...When they put me to death, I'll die remembering the Freedom and Pleasure of My Life. I'll die knowing that there are others coming along to take my place - and most of them won't never get caught.'

...after reading the manuscript of his 'ghosted' autobiography, shortly before his execution:

'Too bad I'm not going to be around long enough for a sequel.'

Jesse Thomas, *from the chair:*

'I'll see you all in hell someday. Let her go!'

William Force, *one of Thomas's partners-in-crime, to the executioner:*

'What are you so nervous about, boy? Take it easy. I'm in no hurry.'

Claude Udwine, *third member of Thomas's killing gang, as he sat in the chair:*

'The good thing about this is that they carry you out – you don't have to walk.'

Jack 'The Hat' McVitie, *urged by Ronnie Kray to 'be a man', and let his twin brother Reggie murder him:*

'I'll be a man, but I don't want to die like one.'

Reggie Kray, *asked on his deathbed why he had killed McVitie:*

'Because he was a vexation to the spirit.'

Pierre-Francois Lacenaire, *French criminal with literary pretensions, as he left for the scaffold:*

'Monsieur Hugo has written a very beautiful book, *The Last Day of a Condemned Man*. But if I had time, I could have beaten him hollow.'

Jack Graham, *American mass-murderer, as he walked to the gas chamber, asked by a reporter if he had any last words:*

'Yeah, I'd like you to sit on my lap as they close the door in there.'

Michel Watrin, *giving his solicitor instructions about leaving his eyes to science, as he went to the guillotine for murdering a taxi driver in 1950:*

'One last request. Can I ask you to be present when they pull out my eyes? Maybe I'll still see you, who knows? That way I'll have more courage.'

Tommy Smithson, *London gangster, as he lay dying in the street from gunshot wounds:*

‘Good morning. I’m dying.’

John Wayne Gacy, *killer of thirty three young men, in a television interview shortly before he went to the gas chamber:*

‘I’m the 34th victim...I believe that after I’m executed, the state will find out that they killed an innocent man.’

...to a guard, as the first of three fatal injections were about to be administered:

‘You can kiss my ass.’

...revellers chanting outside Stateville Correctional Centre, Joliet, following the execution of Gacy, who’d been a children’s entertainer:

‘Turn that frown upside down, they have just fried the clown.’

Peter Kurton, *the Vampire of Dusseldorf, to a prison psychiatrist, shortly before going to the guillotine:*

‘After my head has been chopped off, will I still be able to hear, at least for a moment, the sound of my own blood gushing from the stump of my neck? That would be the pleasure to end all pleasures.’

Frank Vitkovic, *Australian mass killer, to police as he leaped to his death from an eleventh floor window:*

‘That will teach you!’

Fred Lowry, *Australian outlaw, as he died from gunshot wounds:*

‘Tell ’em I died game.’

Sam Bass, *19th Century train robber, to a Texas Ranger who questioned him as he lay dying of gunshot wounds:*

‘If a man knows anything he ought to die with it in him.’

Ned Kelly, *Australian bushranger, as he stood on the scaffold at Melbourne in 1880:*

‘Ah well, I suppose it had to come to this. Such is life.’

Cherokee Bill Goldsby, *killer of thirteen men in Texas in the late 19th Century, asked on the scaffold if he had anything to say:*

‘I came here to die, not to make a speech.’

Bibliography

Abbott J., *In the Belly of the Beast*, Hutchinson, 1982
Allsop K., *The Bootleggers*, Hutchinson, 1961
Anastasia G., *Blood and Honour*, Zebra, NYC, 1993
Audett B., *Rap Sheet*, Cassell, 1955
Bailey B., *Hangmen of England*, WH Allen, 1989
Bailey F.Lee with Aronson H., *The Defence Never Rests*, M.Joseph, 1972
Ball J., Chester L. & Perrott R., *Cops and Robbers*, Penguin, 1979
Bean J.P., *Over The Wall*, Headline, 1994
Bean J.P. *The Sheffield Gang Wars*, D&D Publications, 1981
Benney M., *Low Company*, P.Davies, 1936
Biggs R., *His Own Story*, M.Joseph, 1981
Biondi Lt.R. & Hecox W., *The Dracula Killer*, Mondo, 1992
Bleksley, P., *Gangbuster*. Blake, 2001
Blumenthal R. & Miller J., *The Gotti Tapes*, Arrow, 1992
Blundell N., *The World's Greatest Crooks and Conmen*, Octopus, 1982
Boar R. & Blundell N., *The World's Most Infamous Murders*, Hamlyn, 1990
Bonanno J., *A Man of Honour*, Deutsch, 1983
Boyle J., *A Sense of Freedom*, Pan, 1977
Brady I, The Gates of Janus. Feral House, 2002
Bressler F., *The Chinese Mafia*, Weidenfield & Nicholson., 1980
Bruce J.Campbell, *Escape From Alcatraz*, Hammond, 1964
Bugliosi V. with Gentry C., *Helter Skelter*, Bantam, 1976
Campbell D., *That Was Business, This Is Personal*, Secker &Warburg 1990
Campbell D., *Underworld*, BBC Books, 1994
Cannon E., *Gangster's Lady*, Yellow Brick, 1993
Cannon J., *Tough Guys Don't Cry*, Magnus, 1983
Carpozi J.R., *Son of Sam – the .44 Caliber Killer*, Manor, 1977
Chalidze V., *Criminal Russia: Crime in the Soviet Union*, Random House N.Y, 1977
Challenor H. & Draper A., *Tanky Challenor*, Cooper, 1990
Chandler B.J., *King of the Mountain*, Northern Illinois Univ. Press, 1988
Chapman P., *Chamber of Horrors*, Constable, 1984
Chester G., *Berserk*, O'Mara, 1993
Clark S. & Morley M., *Murder in Mind*, Boxtree, 1993
Collins H., *Autobiography of a Murderer*, Macmillan 1997
Collins H., *Walking Away*, Rebel Inc. 2000
Courtney D., *Stop The Ride, I Want to Get Off*, Virgin 1999.
Cox M., *The Confessions of Henry Lee Lucas*, Warner, 1992
Cullen T., *The Mild Murderer*, Houghton Mifflin, USA, 1977
Deeson A.F.L., *Great Swindlers*, Foulsham, 1971
Delano A., *Slip-Up*, Deutsch, 1977

Dickson J.,Murder Without Conviction, Sphere, 1988
Donaghue A. & Short M., *The Krays' Lieutenant*, Smith Gryphon, 1995
Dyomin M., *The Day is Born in Darkness*, Knopf, N.Y., 1976
Eddy P., Sabogal H. & Walden S., *The Cocaine Wars*, Century, 1988
Elias D., *College Harry*, Longmans, Green &Co., 1957
Eppolito L. & Drury B., *Mafia Cop*, Simon &Schuster, 1992
Ewing C. P., *Kids Who Kill*, Mondo, 1993
Fabian R., *Fabian of the Yard*, Heirloom, 1955
Falcone G. & Padovani M., *Men of Honour*, Fourth Estate, 1992
FF 8282, *A Prison Diary*, Macmillan, 2002
Fielder M. & Steele P., *Alibi at Midnight*, Everest, 1974
Flynn S. & Yeates P., Smack, Gill and Macmillan,1985
Forbes G. & Meehan P., Such Bad Company, Paul Harris, 1982
Fordham R., The Robbers' Tale, Hodder & Stoughton, 1965
Foreman F with Lisners J. Respect. Century 1996
Frank G., The Boston Strangler, Pan, 1967
Frankos D., as told to Hoffman W. & Headley L., Contract Killer, Warner, 1993
Fraser F. with Morton J. Mad Frank's Diary, Virgin, 2000
Fraser F., with Morton J., Mad Frank, Little Brown, 1994
Galante P. & Sapin L., The Marseilles Mafia, WH Allen, 1979
Gaskins D., as told to Earle W., Final Truth, Mondo, 1993
Gaute J. & Odell R., Lady Killers, Granada, 1980
Gaute J.H.H. & Odell R., Murder Whereabouts, Harrap, 1986
Gentry C., J.Edgar Hoover, The Man and his Secrets, Norton, 1991
Gerould D., Guillotine, Blast Books, NYC, 1992
Giancana S. & C., Double Cross, Macdonald, 1992
Goodman D.,Villainy Unlimited, Pan, 1957
Gosch M. & Hammer R., The Luciano Testament, Pan, 1976
Green J.,The Directory of Infamy:The Best of the Worst, Mills & Boon, 1980
Green S., Rachman, M.Joseph, 1979
Grierson F., Famous French Crimes, Muller, 1959
Guerin E., Crime - The Autobiography of a Crook, John Murray,1928
Gugliotta G. & Leen J., Kings of Cocaine, Simon &Schuster, 1989
Habe H., Gentlemen of the Jury, Harrap, 1967
Hamilton C., Men of the Underworld, Gollancz, 1953
Harrison F., Brady & Hindley, Ashgrove Press, 1986
Hercules T., Labelled a Black Villain, Fourth Estate, 1989
Hill B., Boss of Britain's Underworld, Naldrett, 1955
Hinds A., *Contempt of Court*, Bodley Head, 1966
Holden A., *The St Albans Poisoner*, Granada, 1976
Honeycombe G., *The Murders of the Black Museum 1870-1970*, Hutchinson, 1982
Hoover J.Edgar, *Persons in Hiding*, Dent,1938
Hyde H.M. & Kisch J.H., *Casebook of Crime*, Barrie &Rockliff, 1962
Hyde H.M., *Crime has its Heroes*, Constable, 1976
Janson H., *Jack Spot*, Moring, 1958
Jennings A., Lashmar P., Simson V., *Scotland Yard's Cocaine Connection*, Cape,1990
Jones B., *Voices from an Evil God*, Blake, 1993
Jones J., *Let Me Take You Down*, Virgin,1993
Jones R.G., *Killer Couples*, Xanadu, 1987
Joy W. & Prior T., *The Bushrangers*, Shakespeare Head Press, Sydney, 1963

Kaplan D. & Dubro A., *Yakusa*, Queen Anne Press, 1987
Katcher L., *The Big Bank-Roll*, Gollancz, 1959
Katz L., *Uncle Frank*, W.H.Allen, 1975
Kennedy L. *A Presumption of Innocence*, Granada, 1977
King M. & Breault M., Preacher of Death, Signet, 1993
Knight R., with Tracey B., Black Knight, Century, 1990
Kobler J., *Capone*, Coronet, 1973
Kray C., *Me and My Brothers*, Grafton, 1988
Kray R. & Kray R., *Our Story*, Sidgwick&Jackson, 1988
Kray R., Born Fighter, Century, 1990
Krishnamma S.R., *Ballad of the Lazy L*, Rani Press, 1994
La Bern A., *Haigh – The Mind of a Murderer*, W.H. Allen, 1973
Lacey R., *Little Man – Meyer Lansky and the Gangster Life*, Century, 1991
Lambrianou T., *Inside the Firm*, Pan, 1992
Lane B. & Gregg W., *The Encyclopedia of Serial Killers*, Headline. 1992
Lane B., *Murder Update*, Robinson, 1991
Lane B., *The 1995 Murder Yearbook*, Headline, 1994
Lane B., *The Encyclopedia of Women Killers*, Headline, 1994
Lewis J.A., *Means to a Kill*, Headline, 1994
Linedecker C.L., *Night Stalker*, Robinson, 1991
Lourie R., *Hunting The Devil*, Grafton, 1993
Maas P., *The Valachi Papers*, Panther, 1970
Macartney W., *Walls Have Mouths*, Gollancz, 1936
Manson C. with Emmons N., *Without Conscience*, Grafton, 1987
Marks, H., *Mr Nice*, Minerva 1997
Mason P. & Burns J., *Criminal Blunders*, Corgi, 1985
Masters B., *Killing For Company*, Cape, 1985
McConnell B., *Holy Killers*, Headline, 1994
McLagan G. & Lowles, N., *Mr Evil*, Blake 2000
McVicar J., *By Himself*, Artnik, 2002
Meehan P., *Innocent Villain*, Pan, 1978
Meek V., *Cops and Robbers*, Duckworth, 1962
Michaud S.G. & Aynesworth H., *The Only Living Witness*, Penguin, 1993
Moldea D.E., *The Hoffa Wars*, Paddington Press, 1978
Morton J., *Bent Coppers*, Little Brown, 1993
Morton J., *Gangland 2*, Little Brown, 1994
Morton J., *Gangland – The Lawyers*, Little Brown 2001
Morton J., *Gangland*, Little Brown, 1992
Murphy R., *Smash and Grab*, Faber &Faber, 1993
Nash J.R., *World Encyclopedia of 20th Century Murder*, Headline, 1992
Nash J.R., *World Encyclopedia of Organised Crime*, Headline, 1993
Nash,J.R., *Compendium of World Crime*, Harrap, 1983
Neville R. & Clarke J., *The Life and Crimes of Charles Sobhraj*, Cape, 1979
Norris J., *Henry Lee Lucas*, Zebra, 1991
Norris J., *The Killer Next Door*, Arrow,1992
O'Brien J. & Kurins A., *Boss of Bosses*, Simon &Schuster, 1991
O'Connor J., *The Eleventh Commandment*, Seagull, 1976
Olsen J., *The Misbegotten Son*, Headline, 1994
O'Mahoney M., *King Squealer*, Sphere, 1978
Parnell, C., *Hell's Prisoner*, Mainstream, 2003

Pasley, F. D., *Al Capone,The Biography of a Self-Made Man*, Faber, 1966
Payne L., *The Brotherhood*, Joseph, 1973
Pearson J., *The Cult of Violence*, Orion 2001
Phelan J., *Jail Journey*, Secker & Warburg, 1940
Phelan J., *Underworld*, Harrap, 1953
Pierrepoint A., *Executioner Pierrepoint*, Harrap, 1974
Pileggi N., *Wiseguy*, Corgi, 1987
Quimby M.J., *The Devil's Emissiaries*, A.S. Barnes & Co., 1969
Radano G., *Walking the Beat*, World Pub Co 1968
Read L. with Morton J., *Nipper*, Warner, 1992
Reynolds, B., *Autobiography of a Thief*, Bantam Press, 1995
Richardson C., *My Manor*, Sidgwick & Jackson, 1991
Samuel R., *East End Underworld*, R&KP. 1981
Schlecter H., *Deviant The Shocking True Story of the Original Psycho*, Pocket, 1989
Schoenberg R.J., *Mr Capone*, Robson, 1993
Sharpe F.D.'Nutty', *Sharpe of the Flying Squad*, Long, 1938
Shawcross T. & Young M., *Men of Honour*, Collins, 1987
Short M., *Crime Inc.*, Methuen, 1984
Short M., *Lundy*, Grafton, 1991
Silverman J., *Crack of Doom*, Headline, 1994
Skelton D. & Brownlie L., *Frightener*, Mainstream, 1992
Slipper J., *Slipper of the Yard*, Sidgwick and Jackson, 1991
Smithson G., *Raffles in Real Life*, Hutchinson, 1930
Spaggiari A., *The Sewers of Gold*, Granada, 1979
Sparks,R., *Burglar to the Nobility*, Barker, 1961
Steele J., *The Bird That Never Flew*, Sinclair-Stevenson, 1992
Sterling C., *Crime Without Frontiers*, Little Brown, 1994
Sterling C., *The Mafia*, Hamilton, 1990
Sterling C., *The Time of the Assassins*, Angus & Robertson, 1984
Stone I., *Clarence Darrow for the Defence*, Four Square, 1966
Sutton W., *Where The Money Was*, Viking, 1976
Symons J., *Horatio Bottomley*, Cresset Press, 1955
Taki, *Nothing to Declare*, Viking, 1991
Talese G., *Honor Thy Father*, Sphere, 1972
Teresa V., *My Life in the Mafia*, Hart-Davis Macgibbon, 1973
Toland J., *The Dillinger Days*, Barker, 1963
Trow M.J., *Let Him Have it Chris*, Constable, 1990
Turkus B. & Feder S., *Murder Inc.*, Four Square, 1957
Viccei V., *Knightsbridge – The Robbery of the Century*, Blake, 1992
Wannam B., *Tell 'Em I Died Game*, Angus&Robertson, 1964
Ward H. with Gray T., *Buller*, Hodder & Stoughton, 1974
Watts M., *The Men in My Life*, Johnson, 1960
Wickstead B., *Gangbuster*, Futura, 1985
Wilson C. & Pitman P., *Encyclopedia of Murder*, Pan, 1984
Wilson C. & Seaman D., *Encyclopedia of Modern Murder*, Pan, 1983
Wisbey M., *Gangsters Moll*, Little Brown, 2001

Index